World Faiths – An Introduction
Paul Oliver

For UK order enquiries: please contact Bookpoint Ltd,
130 Milton Park, Abingdon, Oxon OX14 4SB.
Telephone: +44 (0) 1235 827720. Fax: +44 (0) 1235 400454.
Lines are open 09.00–17.00, Monday to Saturday, with a 24-hour
message answering service. Details about our titles and how to order
are available at www.teachyourself.com

For USA order enquiries: please contact McGraw-Hill Customer
Services, PO Box 545, Blacklick, OH 43004-0545, USA.
Telephone: 1-800-722-4726. Fax: 1-614-755-5645.

For Canada order enquiries: please contact McGraw-Hill Ryerson
Ltd, 300 Water St, Whitby, Ontario L1N 9B6, Canada.
Telephone: 905 430 5000. Fax: 905 430 5020.

Long renowned as the authoritative source for self-guided
learning – with more than 50 million copies sold worldwide –
the **Teach Yourself** series includes over 500 titles in the fields of
languages, crafts, hobbies, business, computing and education.

British Library Cataloguing in Publication Data: a catalogue record
for this title is available from the British Library.

Library of Congress Catalog Card Number: on file.

First published in UK 2001 by Hodder Education, part of
Hachette UK, 338 Euston Road, London NW1 3BH.

First published in US 2001 by The McGraw-Hill Companies, Inc.

This edition published 2010.

Previously published as Teach Yourself World Faiths

The **Teach Yourself** name is a registered trade mark of
Hodder Headline.

Typeset by MPS Limited, A Macmillan Company.

Printed in Great Britain for Hodder Education, an Hachette UK
Company, 338 Euston Road, London NW1 3BH, by CPI Cox &
Wyman, Reading, Berkshire RG1 8EX.

The publisher has used its best endeavours to ensure that the URLs for
external websites referred to in this book are correct and active at the
time of going to press. However, the publisher and the author have
no responsibility for the websites and can make no guarantee that a
site will remain live or that the content will remain relevant, decent or
appropriate.

Hachette UK's policy is to use papers that are natural, renewable
and recyclable products and made from wood grown in sustainable
forests. The logging and manufacturing processes are expected to
conform to the environmental regulations of the country of origin.

Impression number   10 9 8 7 6 5 4 3 2 1

Year   2014 2013 2012 2011 2010

Contents

Meet the author

Welcome to *World Faiths – An Introduction*!

I have always been fascinated by the different religions which are found around the world. There are two main reasons for this. The first is that religion is usually connected to the culture of people, to their history and sometimes to their political system. In other words, religion is not an isolated phenomenon, but something intimately connected with all aspects of people's lives. The second reason is that religions try to respond to the really profound questions of life – the questions that seem to be fundamental to all human beings. Why do we exist? What is the purpose of our short life? By what principles should we live our life? What happens after death? What should we choose to do with our life? Is the universe just a scientific accident, or is it directed by a divine being?

I am sure we would all love to know the answers to these questions! However, they are not the kind of questions for which the answers can be found outside ourselves. To have any idea about an answer we need to search within ourselves. The religions of the world are a testament to those people who have tried to do just that. They have reflected, meditated and searched within for answers to these great questions of existence. Sometimes the answers may not be entirely satisfactory, but we can feel inspired by the attempt of people to resolve these great questions of life. By studying religion, we also follow in their footsteps, trying to understand these questions as best we can. I hope this book will provide some small assistance on your search.

Paul Oliver, 2010

Only got a minute?

It is often suggested that in many parts of the world there is a diminishing interest in religion. The usual explanation is that in a post-modern society, the world is becoming more and more driven by a desire for consumer goods, and that this materialism is generally more attractive to people than religion. In other words, it is asserted that people are looking to the world outside themselves for gratification, rather than to the interior world of the spirit. While there may be some truth in this, there is also much evidence that interest in religion is not only surviving, but thriving. It may be, however, that this interest in things spiritual is going through a process of fairly rapid evolution. During the nineteenth century, and for most of the twentieth century, people tended to have very little choice in terms of religious practice. They tended to adopt the religion of the society into which they were born. However, with the rapid expansion of communications technology, people have realized that they do have choices. They can easily find many different outlets for their spirituality. Hence people attend meditation classes, yoga classes, non-denominational prayer meetings, spiritual churches, as well as many different forms of religious practice within the main world faiths. In addition, the need for a variety of religious practice has generated a range of different religious organizations and meeting places. In other words, interest in religion may not be diminishing, but simply diversifying. There is thus perhaps the need for books such as the present one, which seek to compare and contrast the range of religions that we find in the world.

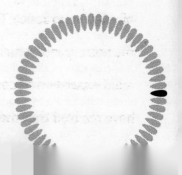

5 Only got five minutes?

A great deal is often said about the apparent differences between religions, and of course, sadly, there have been many violent conflicts down the ages, based upon perceived or actual doctrinal differences between faiths. One could argue, however, that very often the origin of such conflicts lay in economic, social or political issues, with religion being used almost as the excuse rather than the cause of the conflict. It is not too difficult to point to differences between religions, even differences that seem to be extremely profound. For example, Jews, Christians and Muslims may find it very difficult to understand a religion such as Buddhism, which does not subscribe to belief in a single, creator God. Indeed, some people might argue that Buddhism does not fulfil the necessary criteria to count as a religion. They may consider that it is more like a psychology of human behaviour. Nevertheless, one can make out a case that the similarities between religions far exceed the differences. To start with, we can take the issue already noted, that all religions set out broadly to answer the same set of fundamental philosophical and religious questions. In other words, there is a common spirit of enquiry, designed to examine fundamental questions of human existence.

Secondly, all religions share a common concern with trying to provide advice on ways in which human beings can address the great moral questions which confront them in their lives. If we take an ethical question such as whether or not abortion is morally acceptable, then we find that all the principal world faiths take an approximately similar approach to it. In short, there is a general acceptance of the principle of the sanctity of human life. There is a generally common accord that it is wrong to terminate a foetus except in exceptional circumstances. Certainly, different religions acknowledge to differing degrees that social and personal circumstances may modify this general principle, but that does not affect the basic ethical belief in the sanctity of life. On a different but related ethical question, that of non-violence and the use of peaceful means wherever possible to resolve issues, there appears to be a general consensus among religions. All faiths seem to subscribe broadly to the principle of peace and non-violence. Some religions, it is true, make this an absolute principle, while others modify it depending upon particular circumstances. The Jain religion attaches great importance to the principle of non-violence, with its adherents making considerable efforts to avoid the possibility of harming or killing even microscopic creatures. Mahatma Gandhi took this principle of non-violence and adapted it to a political context, applying it to situations where he was faced with people of an opposing viewpoint to his own. Some other religions, such as Christianity, while supporting the principle of non-violence, forgiveness and the use of peaceful means, do appear to concede the use of violence in exceptional circumstances, and to as limited an extent as possible. In general, however, one can discern a shared belief in the morality of non-violence throughout the different religions.

Another apparently shared aspect of religions is the presence in most traditions of a mystical aspect to the faith. Mysticism is a difficult term to define, but points to the desire in human beings to have a direct and intimate relationship with God, or the divine spirit of the universe, depending upon the way in which the individual conceives of their religious belief. Quite apart from the mystical trend appearing to exist to varying degrees in all religions, it is also interesting that mystics tend to use similar techniques in different religions. It is common to employ various forms of meditation and breathing exercises, the chanting of prayers and mantras, and the use of contemplation and spiritual reflection. It is difficult to understand precisely the way in which members of different religions conceive of the mystical goal, but it is very interesting that this appears to be an almost universal religious trend. In other words, although religions may appear, in terms of doctrine, to be rather different, the argument can be made that there are great similarities between the world's faiths.

10 Only got ten minutes?

If we consider so-called primitive religions, such as those associated
with the indigenous peoples of North America or Australia, we
can discern certain features which may indicate something of the
evolution of patterns of belief and worship. There is first of all
a vision of the place of human beings in the universe, the way
in which humans are perceived as relating to the natural world.
There is often also the idea of a spirit world which exists beyond
the physical world, yet is connected to it. Out of these ideas
emerge certain spiritual concepts, often linked to ceremonies and
rituals which help the individual to be in contact with the world
of the spirit or of ancestors. One aspect, however, that is broadly
characteristic of this belief system is that the world of 'religion' is
not necessarily thought of as distinct from the world of 'everyday
life'. The two are seen as intimately connected. Although there
may be holy places which are respected and maintained by the
tribe, these are very different from a modern church or temple,
which is distinct from the institutions of the secular world. In the
tribal context, religion may not even exist as a separate entity from
everyday life. Everything that the tribe encounters in the natural
world may be regarded as spiritual or as reflecting the religious
life. In addition, although there may well be tribal spiritual
leaders, mystics or shamans, they are not typically associated
with the formation of the religion. The life of the spirit is seen
as having existed typically since the beginning of the tribe, since
time immemorial. Although there are generalizations here, we can
contrast this situation with religious life in the contemporary age.

One difference is that there appears to be a greater emphasis upon
the organization of religious experience. Although one can argue
that religions are in many cases thoroughly integrated with the
ordinary lives of people, nevertheless many of the major world
faiths have a complex administrative and bureaucratic system
to support them. There is the danger that these organizational
structures can sometimes distance the religion from its members.

One distinct feature of such organizational systems is the existence of large places of worship which are far removed from the idea of worship in a 'primitive' tribal system. Even if we look back to the origin of religions such as Christianity or Buddhism, we see in the lives of the founders a simplicity far removed from the great buildings associated with the religions today. The original Buddha, Siddhartha Gautama, led the life of a wandering religious mendicant, both before and after his enlightenment. When he became the Buddha, he walked from place to place in northern India, delivering sermons about his teaching, and receiving alms donations from those willing to give food. It was an extremely simple life, not dissimilar to that of Jesus, in a different place and time. Such religious teachers had no great bureaucracy to support them, simply a few disciples and followers, who no doubt provided a small degree of physical support in order that their teacher could continue with his work. Such a simple, spiritual existence contrasts enormously with the large-scale architecture, the complex hierarchies and roles, and the infrastructure of some of the major world faiths today. In order to understand contemporary religious experience, one has at least partly to understand the bureaucratic structures that support them. In each chapter of this book, devoted to a specific faith, there are sections on the history of the religion, and also on its organization. These sections try to describe and analyse the development and evolution of the religion, from its often very simple beginnings.

There is an attempt, for example, to analyse and explain the roles of the leaders of religions, and to try to show to whom members of faiths can turn for a definitive statement of the faith or interpretation of the key teachings. This differs considerably between religions. For example, in Sikhism and in Islam, a holy book holds a pre-eminent position in the religion in terms of providing a definitive statement of religious belief. This is different from say Catholicism, in which although the Bible is very important, the role of the Pope is very much to interpret Christian teachings. The sections on the organization of each religion also explore the different roles that are held within the religion. In most contemporary religions there is a form of hierarchical structure.

Perhaps this is inevitable, given the scale of religious organizations and the very practical matters of administering them and, indeed, of managing the often substantial amounts of money associated with them. Religions are sometimes also divided into clergy and laity, a distinction which some religions find useful or perhaps essential, but which other faiths such as Sikhism have not adopted.

One feature of organized religion historically is that it has tended to be male-dominated. Attempts to reverse this have often given rise to contention, and continue to do so. In some ways religious organizations seem to be very little different from the remainder of society in their apparent reluctance to distribute power and authority equally between men and women. In the early days of the main world religions, there were clear gender divisions in society in terms of social roles. It was also perhaps less easy for women to lead the wandering life of a spiritual mendicant than it was for a man. Nevertheless, very little changed throughout the history of organized religion, until the advent of the social changes, and demands for gender equality in society in general, which arose in the twentieth century. It started to become more and more difficult for religious organizations to resist the argument that, if gender equality was needed in society at large, why not within religious organizations? Although changes are being made, albeit slowly, there is still resistance to gender equality within some religions.

Another interesting feature of world faiths is the development of new religious movements. In a sense, all religions which started at a particular time in history were once new religious movements. However, that term tends to be employed in relation either to groups who have broken away from mainstream religions, or to completely new groups which are theologically or ideologically different from any other religion. Some so-called 'new' religious movements have in fact been established for many years, while others are a recent phenomenon. Several examples of new religious movements are discussed in the book. One interesting aspect of such movements is that they do indicate the need among human beings to find a means of expressing spiritual feelings in a manner that seems suitable to them. This has led in the contemporary world to a considerable expansion in the number of new religions and new spiritual movements, aided to a considerable degree by the ability of such groups to contact people easily using new technology. Some new religious movements are in fact redevelopments of very ancient belief systems. Long before the advent of Christianity, there were various indigenous belief systems in Europe, which Christians later tended to describe as 'pagan'. The latter became to some extent a pejorative term, and such religions were often suppressed. There has been, however, a resurgence of interest in such forms of spirituality, which are often related very closely to the natural world, and this has led to forms of so-called neo-paganism. This is an example of a 'new' religious movement which is not really new, but an attempt to recapture a very ancient tradition.

Although much is made of our secular, materialist society, religion appears to retain a position of significance. This is not really surprising when we consider that religion expresses our deepest feelings about the world, and the factors that tend to motivate and influence our behaviour. Whether or not people regard themselves as belonging to a specific religion, they are usually affected by considerations that are essentially religious or spiritual in nature, and hence the idea of a religious dimension to life seems destined to remain with us, and to occupy an important place in our lives.

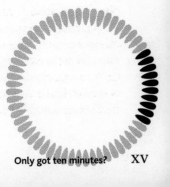

1

Introduction: relationships
between religions

In this chapter you will learn about:
- *the wide variety of religious belief systems*
- *the characteristics of religious belief*
- *ethical principles within religions*
- *mystical aspects of world religions.*

It seems to be a characteristic feature of human existence to sense
that life has a spiritual dimension. This may manifest itself in terms
of membership of one of the major world faiths or it may simply
be that a person feels vaguely that there is 'more to life' than
merely acquiring material possessions and meeting the physical
requirements of existence. Where people are members of a major
faith, then there are often certain expectations of the way in which
they will behave. We perhaps assume that they will read certain
religious texts; that they may pray to a deity or deities; that they
will participate in certain religious rituals; that they will attend
certain ceremonies at a place devoted to communal worship; and
that they may subscribe to a particular code of ethical conduct.
By the same token, those individuals who do not belong to a
mainstream religious tradition may still have strong religious or
spiritual feelings. They may, for example, have a deep sense of the
continuity of life, beyond their own particular span of existence.
They may see their own life as being part of a continuum, so that
even though it has a definite beginning and end, it exists as part of

a broader spectrum of universal existence which is separate from the purely physical, inanimate world. They may also have a sense of sharing a spiritual existence with other human beings. This may be in the sense that they believe that all human beings have certain common experiences as part of the nature of being human.

In short then, many people experience a spiritual dimension to life, whether or not they are part of an organized faith. This spiritual dimension can be contrasted with the secular approach to life, which is characterized in a typical sense by a preoccupation with the material things of life and satisfying the physical requirements of sustaining life. This is not to say, however, that there is a clear dividing line between what we might call the 'spiritual' and the 'secular'. Listening to music, for example, may on one level be purely about physical enjoyment and appear to have no relationship to the spiritual life. Contrariwise, someone who listens to music which s/he really enjoys may experience a lifting of the spirit and an enhanced feeling about life very close to a spiritual experience which we might term 'religious'.

Insight

There are many different terms used to describe feelings of religious experience. These include a sense of the 'mystical' or a feeling of unity with the divine. Whether we speak of spiritual experience or religious experience, all of these terms may point to a universal need in human beings to understand something of the world beyond our physical existence.

The distinction between the spiritual and the secular may in fact be a feature of contemporary society, rather than a long-standing historical phenomenon. In present-day society it is perfectly possible for someone to lead their life totally divorced from a sense of the spiritual. Such a person may successfully earn a living, have a house and car and rear well-adjusted children, without having any sense of the spiritual as part of their life. If a person is happy and feels that s/he leads a fulfilled life, then perhaps it is not completely clear why one might assume that they should have a religious dimension to their life. Although today it seems possible to make a decision to lead a purely secular life, in earlier societies this was much less usual.

In Shinto, the indigenous religion of Japan, there was originally no separate 'name' for Shinto. It only later became known as 'Shinto' to distinguish it from the newer religion of Buddhism. The fundamental reason for the lack of a distinguishing name originally was that Shinto was so much a part of everyday life there was no reason to distinguish a religious life from a secular life. *Kami*, or spirits, were seen as part of the natural world of trees, mountains and rivers and also as part of family ancestors. The entire world was a spiritual, religious world. Arguably there are parallels with Christian European society in the Middle Ages, and certainly with traditional Hindu society. One might also argue that there is a similar situation with regard to the world view of indigenous Americans or Australians. Both groups of people had (and have) a sophisticated relationship with the natural world, which was fundamentally spiritual.

The range of religious beliefs

When we consider societies in which the secular and the spiritual are very closely intertwined, it becomes far less easy to define clearly what we mean by the 'religious'. It is perhaps far easier to achieve this distinction when we consider contemporary society. Certainly as we consider the range of world faiths, it is evident that there are enormous variations in patterns of belief and worship.

There are first of all faiths that have no deity to which people pray or carry out devotions. Perhaps the largest religion which comes into this category is Buddhism. To the uninitiated, Buddhists may *appear* to be worshipping the Buddha. After all, tourists may visit Buddhist temples in Thailand and see large golden statues of the Buddha at the front of a temple, much as there may be a large statue of the crucifixion in a Christian church. Although appearances may be to the contrary, there is no sense in which the Buddha is 'worshipped' as a deity. The Buddha is seen as a spiritually enlightened human being whose teaching is capable, if followed diligently, of helping human beings to reduce the suffering inherent in their lives. In terms of the statue of the Buddha, this is seen as an image of an enlightened person meditating and as such as a reminder of the teaching of the Buddha and of the potential inherent in all human beings to reduce suffering. A Buddhist would not normally, according to the teaching, pray to the Buddha for help in solving problems in life. A Buddhist would not, for example, pray for a miracle or for divine intervention in some form. The Buddhist would reflect upon the teachings of the Buddha, perhaps using the statue as a form of inspiration for what was, in fact, possible in life. Neither the Buddha image nor the historical Buddha himself is seen as any kind of deity. They are merely a reminder of the spiritual achievements of one human being and the way in which today Buddhists may utilize those achievements to improve the quality of their lives.

Insight

It is worth recognizing that in many religions there is usually a great diversity of practice. The culture of a country may interact with religious belief to produce a range of practice which may differ from that in a different cultural environment.

The situation in Christianity is very different from in Buddhism. Christians may pray to Jesus Christ, asking Him to intervene in the world to help them. Buddhists are entirely dependent upon their own efforts to help bring about a change in the world or to reduce their own suffering. Christians, by Contrast, besides their own efforts, would see the possibility that through their faith in God, God would be able, in principle, to intervene and help them in their lives. Christianity shares a clearly monotheistic world view with Islam, Judaism and Sikhism, among others. This is not to say, of course, that members of these different faiths have the same perception of the deity in their particular religion; only that they subscribe to the view that there is a single deity. Some other faiths, such as Taoism, appear to subscribe to the view not that a deity as such exists, but rather that there is a spiritual force influencing the universe and that it is possible, in principle, for Taoists to acquire a close understanding of the nature of that spirit. In other religious systems such as Confucianism, the relationship between the Confucian world view and the existence or otherwise of a deity is perhaps slightly less than clear.

Thus there are faiths that are clearly monotheistic in terms of belief in a single, all-powerful God and there are other faiths which appear not to subscribe to the existence of a deity as such. There are also, however, faiths that appear to combine some elements of both of these positions, having both personal deities to which the individual person may make approaches and also the rather impersonal universal spirit which has a unifying influence over the whole of existence.

Hinduism is perhaps an example of this position. There are many individual deities in Hinduism, so much so that a newcomer to the study of the faith may be rather bewildered at the multiplicity of images of deities found in that religion. Among the more common deities are Krishna, Shiva, Sarasvati and Ganesh, the god with the appearance of an elephant. It is worth noting that the worship of these personal gods is not something which takes place solely on the occasions when someone visits the temple. On the contrary, images of the gods are to be found in all areas of society. A hairdresser who has set up a small stall on the streets of an Indian city may well surround his workplace with framed pictures of his favourite deities. Such pictures are often mass-produced and a common sight in Indian cities. Taxi drivers will also typically have many small images of deities on the fascia of their vehicles, beside the steering wheel. An individual deity is often associated with a particular dimension of life, and prayers will be offered to that god or goddess at appropriate times. The important feature of this approach to deities is that it permeates many facets of life, producing a blurring of the distinction between the religious and the secular.

Although one can view these gods and goddesses as being immanent and very close to the day-to-day lives of people, one can also see them as manifestations of a more general religious force. The universal spirit or Brahman of the Upanishads can be viewed as the spiritual force which influences all of the living and inanimate world. All of the immanent, personal gods can be seen as a part of such a universal spirit. On this rather more philosophical plane, the absolute can be seen as a divine element in everyone. It may well be true that many people in their daily lives are not in a state of regular reflection on Brahman, but the more personal deities of Hinduism offer a straightforward approach to religious experience which is available in daily life.

Insight

While Hinduism is often thought of as involving belief in many gods and goddesses, on a more philosophical, abstract plane it can be considered as a religion of a single divine entity, Brahman.

Similarities between world faiths

It is relatively easy to find differences between world faiths and, indeed, such differences are so numerous that such an analysis could proceed for a long time. It is probably a more complex task to look for similarities between religions or at least for shared themes that characterize the spiritual life.

If we are to draw a distinction between the religious life and the secular life, then it is a reasonable assumption that there must be questions and issues that are distinctively 'religious', and this certainly seems to be the case. Religions, for example, generally appear to address the possibility of an existence beyond the present, earthly lifespan of a human being. In Christianity, for example, there is the clear promise of a 'life after death'. For the Christian who has faith in God and makes a sincere attempt to live life according to the example and precepts of Jesus Christ, there is the promise of eternal life, close to God the Father in heaven. In Hinduism and Jainism, the prospect of an existence in a spiritual realm after the earthly existence is linked to concepts of *karma*, reincarnation and the doctrine of the cycle of birth, death and rebirth. The assumption of karma is that the deeds of an individual accrue certain consequences which have to be lived through in future existences, until all the consequences have been eliminated. Only then can the individual achieve release from the cycle of reincarnation. In Jainism, the main method for eliminating the results of karma is to lead an ascetic life.

Some religions, therefore, tend to offer an analysis of the nature of existence after a physical death and also offer a spiritual 'path' along which the individual may travel in order to achieve a new spiritual existence after death. Buddhism, however, offers a rather different analysis of this issue. It certainly acknowledges the validity of the question, since it is recorded that the Buddha in his lifetime was asked this question by one of his disciples. He chose not to respond directly to the question of the nature of an afterlife. His answer was that the question itself is unimportant. His argument was that the only truly important issue is the manner in which we live our present lives. This should be our total preoccupation. In other words, human beings should devote themselves to the system of mental training set out by the Buddha and should adopt this in order to try to reduce the suffering in their lives. The principle of mindfulness enunciated by the Buddha exhorted people to concentrate on life in the present and to live each moment in a sensitive and careful manner. One might perhaps summarize the Buddhist view by saying that the only reality is the present.

Nevertheless, one can see that conjectures about the nature of further possible existences are characteristic of religious faiths. Religion also shares much in common with philosophy, and religious and philosophical questions are often fairly similar. Another area which is central to the religious life is the question of the nature of reality. In philosophical terms this can be referred to as an ontological question. If it is applied to spiritual matters, it raises such issues as whether the material, day-to-day world is compatible with the religious life or whether true spirituality may only be found in some 'otherworldly' existence which is distinct from the ordinary daily life of, for example, earning a living and raising a family. This is very much connected with questions of religious lifestyles. Some people may argue, for example, that the religious life should really be lived 'in the world' as a part of ordinary, daily existence, while others may suggest that the truly religious life is one of contemplation and withdrawal from the world.

The responses to this important question are different in separate religious traditions, but it is an issue which emerges in all faiths. In the Sikh religion, for example, there has always been an emphasis upon the importance of integrating the spiritual life with day-to-day living. This was always emphasized by Guru Nanak, the founder of the Sikh religion. In his later years at Kartarpur, he continued to earn his living as a farmer, as if to stress the significance of the importance of daily labour. In addition, at one point in the early history of Sikhism, the Sikhs would not accept converts to the faith from *sadhus* and *sannyasins* who were leading a life dependent upon alms given by others.

One might also reflect upon whether the practical approach to life which is characteristic of the Sikh faith was also affected to some degree by the location of Panjab. This area of the Indian subcontinent is situated on the main trade and also invasion route into India from the Asian steppes. The route through the Khyber Pass led directly through Panjab, and this resulted in the Sikhs frequently finding themselves in the centre of a region affected by war and conflict. Perhaps in order for them to survive in such a situation, it was necessary to act in the world, rather than to adopt an 'otherworldly' approach.

Other faiths have also to varying degrees seen it as important to respond to the world as they found it. Confucianism was very much an ethical approach to the practical questions of daily life, so much so that after the death of Confucius, his approach was gradually adopted by the political and administrative systems in China. Some traditions such as Zen Buddhism, which are sometimes considered as withdrawing from the world, also have a practical element in their practice. Zen monks are frequently required to do a considerable amount of manual work as part of their training regime, the purpose of this being partly a training in mindfulness, but also in being non-attached to other activities in which perhaps sometimes they would rather be engaged. Judaism is also very much a life-affirming tradition. There is much less of the emphasis upon withdrawal from the world than there is in some other faiths. Judaism emphasizes family life and indeed many of the traditions of Judaism are as much centred on the family as they are on the synagogue.

Nevertheless, there are a number of world faiths which respond to the basic ontological question about the spiritual nature of the world in a broadly different manner. Some faiths, or at least traditions within those faiths, view the material world as fundamentally unsatisfactory in a spiritual sense and consider that the most appropriate means of religious expression is to withdraw from the world in some way.

Insight

In many religious traditions, there exists the practice of withdrawal from the world. Those who adopt this style of life are often a source of inspiration for lay people who live and work in the everyday world.

There is, of course, a long monastic tradition within Christianity, which reached its highest development in medieval times in Europe, but whose antecedents may be traced back to those people who, in the centuries following the death of Jesus, found their spiritual life in desert communities. The contemplative life is certainly found within the Sufi tradition in Islam, and also within Taoism in China. Perhaps, however, it is within Hinduism and Buddhism that one finds the clearest examples of withdrawal from the world.

The ideal of the religious recluse occurs in many different contexts in Hinduism. The general theme is of the person who retires from the cares of the world, living in an isolated location, leading a life devoted to meditation and contemplation. This is usually accompanied by a very simple lifestyle, perhaps living on food alms given by disciples. The *guru*, or teacher, may have one or two disciples who are trained in yoga and the scriptures by the guru and who later assume an independent, similar way of life. The discipline of yoga and meditation may also be accompanied by the practice of various austerities. These might include sitting or standing in various difficult postures for long periods of time (sometimes for periods of years); submitting to being buried for periods of time; and perhaps also the self-denial of food and water for periods. Such austerities are claimed to help with attaining spiritual insights.

Lifestyles of this type are to varying degrees described and advocated in scriptures such as the *Bhagavad Gita* and the Upanishads. The mendicant lifestyle is also regarded as part of the ideal type of Hindu life stages or *ashramas*. The basic stages of the idealized Hindu life conclude with the person withdrawing from family life and living a reclusive life in the forest, finally leaving to become a wandering *sadhu*.

Neither is this approach to the spiritual life merely something of historical interest. The lifestyle of the wandering mendicant is very much in existence in contemporary India. *Sadhus* are a frequent sight in India, coming together in very large gatherings at events such as the Kumbh Mela.

Similarly in Theravada Buddhism, the monks and nuns lead a fairly austere lifestyle. Although the system advocated by the historical Buddha is often referred to as the Middle Way, to many people the monastic way of life would seem quite strict and lacking in many of the comforts of life. The way of life in Buddhist monasteries in Europe is modelled on that in South-east Asia. The monks and nuns rise at about 5.30 or 6.00 a.m. and attend the main meditation hall for chanting from the Pali scriptures, followed by a lengthy period of meditation. There is then a breakfast of porridge and tea. There is only one main meal during the day, taken at noon. After that no food is consumed at all until the breakfast of the following day.

Ordained monks and nuns have only a few very basic possessions such as a robe and a bowl in which they can collect food alms.

They are not supposed to handle money and hence do not have the means simply to go out and satisfy any need that makes itself felt. The entire purpose of the lifestyle is to ensure that monks and nuns only have the very basic essentials which are required to sustain life. After that, they are trained to adjust to whatever is available and to accept life the way it is. It would be possible for them to ask for things such as medicines if they were ill, but in general terms they are not encouraged to ask for something simply because it would create a temporary feeling of happiness or pleasure. They have very basic living and sleeping accommodation, which may consist of a simple hut or room, and when they receive their midday meal, they should accept whatever is given, rather than showing any satisfaction, pleasure or indeed disappointment. They certainly are not supposed to ask for any particular kind of food to be included in the meal, simply because they enjoy eating that food.

Similarly, in working around the monastery, they are encouraged to do whatever work is required, rather than seeking out a particular kind of work which they find fulfilling or pleasurable. They should accept eagerly and with gratitude any work which they are asked to complete. In other words, they are not encouraged to try to mould the external world to make it pleasanter for them or more satisfying. Rather, they are encouraged to be accepting of the world as it is.

Many Buddhist monasteries are involved in community work of various kinds, in teaching and in writing. They do not, then, withdraw from the world in quite the same way as Hindu *sadhus*. Nevertheless, the material world is seen as ultimately unsatisfactory and unsatisfying. It is the antithesis of Buddhism to try always to make the world more pleasant. The Buddhist is perhaps not so much trying to change the world or to withdraw from it, but rather to accept it as it is and to purify the human response to that imperfect world.

Another fundamentally religious question which the different faiths attempt to answer is the nature of the ultimate power and authority in the universe. The religions that have all developed just to the east of the Mediterranean, i.e. Judaism, Christianity and Islam, all possess the concept of a single, all-powerful god, who created the universe as we know it. Likewise Sikhism has the concept of a single god.

Some other faiths are rather different in their concept of the power controlling the universe. Buddhism has no concept of a divinity and, in fact, does not really address the question. Buddhism has really no sense of the metaphysical and concentrates very much on what we might reasonably regard as the psychology of the individual person attempting to respond to the challenges of an imperfect world.

Some other faiths adopt a somewhat intermediate position between monotheism and the negation of any deity. These faiths, such as Taoism and Shinto, conceptualize the universe as being under the influence of a spiritual force, which in Taoism is known as the Tao and which in Shinto would probably be seen as the spiritual source of the *kami* or multiplicity of spirits which exist in the world. One might also include in this broad perspective the Brahman of the Upanishads in Hinduism.

The concept which a particular faith has of the power and authority over the universe affects many aspects of religious practice. Not least, for instance, it affects the nature of prayer in that faith. It is perhaps less easy to pray to an abstract spiritual force than it is to pray to a personal deity. The other aspect of this question is that even if two religions claim a similar concept of a deity, there is no way of knowing in any absolute sense the actual idea of the deity which is carried around in the mind of the devotee. One can perhaps seek the empirical evidence of people who have described their religious experiences. This might provide some idea of the nature of the concept of God, but it is far from clear how one might attempt an accurate analysis and description of the manner in which deities are conceptualized.

Differences in the concept of God are perhaps just one way in which religions have clashed over the centuries. It is undoubtedly sad that religion, encapsulating as it does a way of life devoted to the highest of ideals, should have been the cause of so much conflict throughout history. Perhaps it is the profound nature of those ideals which, ironically, is at the heart of religious conflict. Religious belief, for example, tends to go to the very heart of how we conceptualize ourselves as human beings. It is often more than simply a set of precepts, and touches on most of the different facets of the way we view the world. When one person meets another individual with a completely different world view, then the outcome may be some degree of conflict. Religions tend to address some of the issues which are, at the same time, the most profound and also the most important to us. Our vision of what happens to us after death is one such issue. Religions differ in terms of regarding this issue as, on the one hand, not being of central importance (e.g. Theravada Buddhism) to, on the other hand, being a central concern for how we live our life on earth (e.g. Christianity). With differences between religions on such central issues it is not difficult to see how tensions can arise.

Religious authority has historically often been connected with secular, political and economic authority. Throughout history, military leaders have often sought religious sanction for the waging of war, and religious leaders have sometimes seen it as one of their proper duties to pronounce on the justness or otherwise of war. Since religious power and political power have sometimes been difficult to disentangle, this has provided another forum within which religions could find themselves in conflict.

Ethics and world faiths

Another important range of questions which are part of a religious framework are those questions about how human beings ought to live their lives. These are fundamentally ethical questions. Ethics can legitimately be regarded as a sphere of study of secular philosophy and yet ethical questions have very much come to be regarded as part of the religious area of knowledge. The main religions have generally set out to delineate certain ways of acting as being acceptable and moral and others as being unacceptable.

Some religions have fairly strict ethical teachings and in Judaism, for example, the *Torah* contains over 600 requirements with which Jews are supposed to comply. In Islam, there are requirements such as *zakat*, which means that Muslims should give to charitable causes what amounts to about two and a half per cent of their annual income and possessions. Muslims may give to deserving causes at other times, but *zakat* is regarded as ritual giving and an obligation upon Muslims. There are thus ethical requirements which are part of a particular religious view and which may be regarded as absolute, in the sense that they are part of the belief system of the faith. The customs within Jainism which are connected with a non-violent perspective on the world might also reasonably be thought of as an example of this perspective. Such customs include the filtering of drinking water to remove any tiny living creatures before drinking and the wearing of gauze over the mouth to prevent the inhalation and therefore killing of small insects and so on.

In some other religious systems, however, ethical thought may be regarded as rather more relativistic. Even then, though, it depends to some extent on where one searches within the range of practice and doctrine which make up the faith as a whole. In Hinduism, for example, one might point to the apparently strict requirements of caste membership as evidence of very clearly defined ethical rules. To that extent, the social structure of Hinduism may be considered to reflect a degree of ethical absolutism.

And yet, in the *Bhagavad Gita*, one of the most widely read Hindu scriptures and beloved of Mahatma Gandhi, there is arguably a slightly more flexible approach to ethics. The book opens with a battle scene, which may well be regarded as a metaphor for the moral dilemmas of life. Arjuna, a Hindu prince, is in his chariot on one side of the battlefield, facing the opposing armies in which he can see personal friends and relatives. He does not wish to fight. This is the scene which is set for Arjuna's charioteer to reflect on the dilemmas which confront human beings. It transpires that the charioteer is none other than the god Krishna. The remainder of the *Bhagavad Gita* is an opportunity for Krishna to expound his philosophy of the way in which human beings should act in the world and can be seen, in effect, as a treatise on Hindu ethics.

Krishna's argument is that there is nothing intrinsically wrong with action or with work, but it is the motive which is important. It is essential, according to Krishna, that people do not have any expectations from their actions. More particularly, they should not have any selfish aspirations from their actions. They should not act in a particular way, simply to hope for a particular reward. On the contrary, all their actions should be dedicated to God. One of the key principles here is that of non-attachment. The true *yogi*, according to the *Gita*, is unattached to the fruits of his or her actions. S/he acts purely from unselfish motives. Krishna argues that the pursuit of pleasure does not lead to happiness, because the pleasures generated by the material, physical world are impermanent. Only the pleasure and peace of mind which arise through unattached action dedicated to God have any degree of permanence.

The *Gita* tends to concentrate on the ultimate motives for actions, rather than on the issues inherent in the choice of one action rather than another. Hence there is a measure of relativity in terms of deciding whether to act in one way rather than another. Presumably, in practical terms, Hindus would feel constrained by the requirements of the caste to which they belonged and hence one might argue that to some extent ethical principles would be normative, conditioned by the requirements and limitations of the immediate social group. There is no general sense in the *Gita* of actions being specifically approved and other actions being specifically prohibited.

This is not quite the same in Buddhism, where there are certain prohibitions, although these are expressed in a fairly general way. The Noble Eightfold Path is the guide enunciated by the historical Buddha to enable human beings to reduce and then eliminate suffering in their lives and to escape from the cycle of birth, death and rebirth.

Of the eight elements to the Buddha's path, three are specifically concerned with the way in which human beings should behave in their day-to-day lives. These are the injunctions to adopt 'Right Speech', 'Right Conduct' and 'Right Livelihood'. It should be noted, however, that there are differences between the interpretation of these requirements for lay Buddhists and for ordained members of the Buddhist *sangha* (monks and nuns). Generally speaking, as one might assume, the expectations of monks and nuns in terms of behaviour are much stricter than for lay Buddhists.

Right Speech is the requirement to abstain from such activities as telling lies about people and engaging in slanderous talk. Generally it is the requirement not to speak unkindly about others. However, the principle of Right Speech also reminds Buddhists that they should not engage in what we might term 'idle chatter'; simply chatting about things in a thoughtless and casual manner. Buddhists are expected to be mindful and aware at all times and this is seen as applying very much to speech.

Right Conduct relates to the principles of not killing other living things and also of not stealing anything. The principle of not taking life applies not only to the act of murder of a human being, but also to not taking the life of any other living creature, however small. It is often extended by Buddhists to the more general principle of caring for all living things and having a mindful awareness of the existence of other life. A Buddhist, for example, would perhaps not idly snap off a leaf or twig from a plant. Although this might not result in the death of the plant, it would be regarded as an unnecessary and unethical action.

Right Livelihood is the principle that lay Buddhists should earn their living by a method that does not entail doing harm to other living things. Thus professions such as hunter, butcher or soldier, which entail killing other living creatures, would be thought unacceptable.

Quite apart from elements of the Noble Eightfold Path, Buddhism also emphazises general ethical behaviour in terms of exhibiting kindness and compassion towards all living things. Here there is an ethical principle which does not normally seek to set down specific rules or obligations, but describes in general terms a state of mind which the Buddhist is asked to cultivate. This is the state in which the individual regards the whole world and particularly other living creatures with a sense of kindness. The *Mettasutta* or *Sutta of Loving Kindness* is the Buddhist scripture which formalizes advice in this area of ethics.

Although, then, there is a sense within Buddhism, and particularly within the Noble Eightfold Path, of a number of ethical 'requirements', they are typically expressed in a fairly general way, which leaves scope for the interpretation of the individual. For example, in terms of the principle of Right Livelihood, there is considerable room for debate about which types of employment might or might not result in suffering to others. There is considerable scope here for individual judgement. Equally, the concepts of loving kindness and of compassion establish basic ethical principles, but leave the detailed application to the reflection and mindfulness of individuals.

Changes in religious commitment

It may or may not be too much of a commonplace to mention, but religions do not remain constant in terms of their popularity with people. Buddhism, for example, started in north-eastern India and southern Nepal and spread relatively rapidly throughout Asia. It has been arguably the principal religious influence throughout eastern Asia, becoming established at different times in China, Tibet, Japan, Thailand, Korea, Sri Lanka and other countries. Nevertheless, it became almost eliminated in India, the country of its origin.

There are other examples. Zoroastrianism was at one time a very widespread and influential religion in Iran and yet other than its retention by a fairly small group of migrants who settled in India (i.e. the Parsis), it has now become very much a minority faith in its country of origin. Islam, from its inception, spread extremely rapidly and has largely retained its influence over the countries where it originally became established. There are one or two minor exceptions, such as the lack of present-day influence of Islam in southern Spain. Confucianism was the 'established' religion of China for a very long time, but changes in the political situation in the country altered that. Similarly, the close link which developed between the cult of the Emperor in Japan and the Shinto religion was extremely strong and yet this was severed after the defeat of Japan in World War II. Again, political changes affected the relationship between an organized religion and the social structure of a country.

Some faiths have been extremely resilient in terms of surviving adversity and conflict with either other religions or different political systems. In India, for example, Hinduism has succeeded in retaining its culture and religious practices despite the rule of the Mughal Empire and the later British Raj. Neither administration in India was uniformly hostile to Hindu culture and religion, yet there remained conflict in some areas. Nevertheless, Hinduism survived and has proved itself very adaptable. Indeed, in some cases, it produced thinkers and philosophers who sought to combine the best of Hindu thought with that of other cultures. Another religion which has proved extremely resilient is Judaism. In this case, one can only marvel at the manner in which the religious culture has been sustained amid the dispersal or diaspora of Jews around the world. The Jewish community has not had the benefit of a stable homeland in which it could consolidate its faith and ensure that the rituals and teachings were maintained. All of this had to be achieved in many different locations around the world and in the context of often the most terrible persecution.

Sikhism is also a faith which has experienced considerable difficulties in its development. These difficulties have partly emerged from the geographical location of Panjab and also from the conflict with other faiths which has taken place from time to time.

The Sikhs are also a religious group who have undergone an extensive degree of migration around the world and yet in whichever area they have settled, they have tended to be very energetic at retaining their culture and in terms of building *gurdwaras*, or Sikh 'temples', which could be the focus for their faith and for the retention of their language (Panjabi) and culture.

Christianity, rather like Buddhism, has not retained a significant presence in the country of its origin and yet has also been very successful in terms of becoming established in other countries and cultures. The popularity and influence of Christianity have also varied enormously throughout history. One can only contrast the political power and influence of Christianity in medieval times with the somewhat dwindling church attendances in some areas today. Nevertheless, Christianity remains a very significant influence, although one can discern changing patterns of commitment.

It is perhaps not surprising that religions do change in their social structures and in some cases doctrinal beliefs, if one accepts the sociological thesis that religions themselves are partly a product of the society in which they develop. In other words, the belief system of a particular faith finds acceptance partly for the very reason that those beliefs are at least not antithetical to that particular culture. Subsequently, when the secular culture changes, it would not be surprising if there were changes in the society's commitment to that particular religion. Within this sort of analysis one would not find it very surprising if, as one religion grew in popularity, another waned in terms of the number of practising adherents.

Mystical elements in world faiths

Within most religions, practitioners seek a direct experience of God or the divine. A variety of techniques may be used to try to achieve this, including prayer and meditation. This approach to religious experience is often referred to as mysticism, although it is not always easy to define precisely where mystical approaches can be differentiated from everyday religious practices. The approach of mystics to try to establish a direct and personal contact with God has sometimes distinguished them from people who approach God through the intercession of an ordained clergy.

The term 'mysticism' is certainly very difficult to define in a precise and all-inclusive manner. This is at least partly because the mystical experience itself is sometimes described as being beyond the capacity of expression in mere words. It is sometimes said that the mystical experience is something which must be felt in a subjective sense, before one can understand it. In other words, it is not completely susceptible to objective, empirical analysis. Hence it is not easy to define a phenomenon which some people find difficult, in any case, to express in words.

The most usual definition of mysticism involves a tradition or religious path whose aim is a union of the individual soul or self with the divine. Mystical experience is also usually described, by those who are able to do so, as involving feelings of great bliss and happiness and also a sense of overwhelming inner peace and harmony. It may also be described as a sense of the individual being able to reach spiritually a realm that would otherwise be inaccessible.

As with all definitions, however, it is rarely easy to encompass all instances of a phenomenon within a fairly short description. There are religious traditions, for example, which one would probably wish to describe as either mystical or at least having strong mystical elements within them, which at the same time do not involve any identification with a god or gods. Jainism is one example of this. Another would be Zen Buddhism. The aim of the latter is that the aspirant should ultimately attain *satori* or gain an enlightenment experience which helps him or her to understand the true nature of reality. The enlightenment experience of Zen Buddhism is certainly not theoretical in nature, but is an experiential understanding of the essential operation of the universe, which affects both the response of the individual to the world in general and also his or her relationships with other human beings. Nevertheless, although the enlightenment experience would typically be described as mystical, there is no sense of a merging of the individual soul with a divinity.

The mystical quest is usually accompanied by a course of spiritual training, which typically incorporates some degree of asceticism or physical denial. To continue a previous example, Zen Buddhist training in a monastic setting is a fairly rigorous endeavour. Sometimes, if an aspirant monk requests to undergo training, he is told that he may not be admitted or that no places are available. This is a technique to test his determination. If he stays and repeats his request, he may ultimately be admitted.

The training involves long and arduous periods of meditation, combined with fairly hard physical work around the monastery. The food is very basic and not designed to stimulate the palate. In some monasteries, lack of attention during meditation sessions or lack of mindfulness and care while carrying out labours around the monastery are rewarded by a sharp slap on the back with a stick, in order quickly to refocus the mind. Sleep is limited and monks have to rise very early in the morning. The general discipline of the monastery is strict and governed by the abbot. From time to time, the abbot will see individual monks to assess their progress with the training and meditation.

The role of the teacher in mystical training is regarded as very important. Gaining mystical understanding is not regarded as simply acquiring a measure of doctrinal knowledge. Mystical understanding, almost by definition, can only be authenticated by someone who has themselves acquired at least that same degree of understanding and spiritual development. There is the assumption in many mystical traditions that the teacher passes on the understanding to the pupil, who, on becoming a teacher, also transmits this understanding. In this way there is a chain of transmission and within some religions it is often a pertinent question to ask a religious teacher the identity of their teacher.

Within Sufism, the teacher is often known as a *shaikh*, while in Hinduism, the term guru is normally used. Within Hinduism, even when the pupil has left his or her guru to lead an independent life, contact is still maintained with the guru. Pupils will return to visit their gurus regularly, partly to receive teaching, but also to care for them if they are elderly. The guru is regarded with great esteem, being perhaps even closer than a parent to a religious mystic. Mystical traditions, such as yoga, are usually learned from a guru or adept.

There is a reasonable degree of commonality concerning the range of techniques used within mystical traditions. A common method involves the use of the *mantram*, or holy syllable, which is repeated over and over again. The steady repetition has perhaps a similar effect to breathing meditation, in that it helps to calm the mind in preparation for other forms of meditation. The use of the *mantram* is widespread, in Hinduism, Buddhism, Sikhism and Sufism. Sometimes the *mantram* will be a name of god; in other faiths, it may be a spiritual word or phrase of a different kind.

Asceticism has been traditionally associated with mystical practice. The assumption here is that a comfortable lifestyle which caters for worldly needs is not necessarily compatible with gaining spiritual insights. Even though the orthodox elements in a faith may not be otherworldly, it is fairly usual for the mystical element in a religion to practise some degree of asceticism or self-denial. Among Hindu ascetics, these may be taken sometimes to what most would regard as extremes of self-mortification. Some *sadhus* or holy men will submit to being buried alive for a number of days. They claim typically that such practices improve their sense of spiritual well-being and help them to gain mystical insights. Living off a very frugal diet is a fairly normal practice, as is the adoption of long periods of meditation practice. Many mystics will live either in a monastic setting, or else will have a very simple dwelling in an isolated, peaceful location. In India, many holy men lead a more or less permanently itinerant life, perhaps only living in one place for a short time during inclement weather.

Although one of the principal features of religions is often considered to be a belief in a deity or deities, there is arguably a more general characteristic of a religious belief system.

This is that it is a belief system in which individuals have a sense of the universe and of their place within it. In other words, their perception of their own lives is not limited to their immediate existence, but rather looks out to a broader world and to the life forms which inhabit it. They also look out to a universe which is currently unknown, but which engenders a feeling of wonderment. Perhaps also there is a sense of trying to explain the universe to oneself and this creates the motivation to look at things from a religious perspective.

Certainly the faiths described in this book all seek to look beyond the immediate existence of human beings to wider horizons. Taoism has no deity and yet is infused with a love of and admiration for the broad, empty expanses of nature. Taoist devotees lived in isolated places, leading lives of meditation and tranquillity. Taoist paintings are often characterized by a sense of space. They typically contain images of high mountain ranges, pine forests, fast-flowing streams and noticeably often a single monk meditating or travelling within this inspiring wilderness. Often the painting has large expanses of sky or of forest, as if the artist is creating a contrast between the tiny solitary human figure and the vastness of the universe.

In Buddhist meditation, one of the aims is to calm the mind and then to ease thoughts from the mind, leaving it empty. One of the characteristics of the mind is that it is continually filled with fluctuating thoughts, coming and going, disturbing the potential tranquillity of the mind. Meditation seeks to help the individual to allow thoughts to come into the mind, but then also to leave the mind and not to remain as the focus of attention. The emptiness and silence of the mind is regarded as a very positive element in Buddhist practice.

Insight

It is sometimes suggested that Buddhism concentrates on the nature of the individual. However, meditation, it is argued, tends to prepare the individual person to have a positive attitude in relating to the external world.

Although Buddhism appears to concentrate on the individual, in the sense that it focuses on the problem of suffering and the strategies which may be employed in eliminating that suffering, it also addresses the nature of existence in a broader universe. Buddhism encourages the individual to try to understand the nature of all existence and, in particular, the characteristics of existence. Thus all existence is seen as being impermanent. This impermanence is seen as applying not only to the lives of individuals, but also to the broader animate and inanimate material in the universe. Thus, trees, mountains, lakes, this planet, the sun and indeed galaxies and the whole universe are seen as being ultimately impermanent. The Buddhist is thus encouraged to look beyond his or her own small-scale existence.

Following on from the concept of impermanence is that of suffering, or 'unsatisfactoriness', to use a typical Buddhist word. We know that the energy of our star, the sun, is certain to expire one day. In other words, it is impermanent. What is more, that impermanence is unsatisfactory. It would be 'better' in many ways if the sun continued shining for ever, and gave future generations of human beings, and future life on earth, a guaranteed existence. But this is not to be. If human beings continue as a species, our rational minds tell us that one day the earth will begin to cool and will not be able to sustain life. This is the unsatisfactory nature of the universe. Things do not go on unchanged for ever.

In our own lives we would perhaps like it if we were able to pick a day when we felt supremely happy and then that day could extend for ever. Perhaps all our family could be around us and we would feel healthy and contented. But we know this cannot be. The Buddhist is encouraged to look at the impermanent and unsatisfactory nature of the world and to accept it in the way that it is. The purpose is at least partly to appreciate that the same forces of existence apply to our own lives as apply at the cosmic level and that there is nothing at all that we can do to alter these basic rules of existence. Although we cannot alter them, what we certainly can do is to alter our attitude to them. We can come to terms with them in a variety of ways.

It does not matter into which culture we are born, there are certain inevitable characteristics of life and the universe with which we must come to terms. Life is created and later ceases to exist. Living things ultimately malfunction and then die. The young grow old and lose their youth. We reflect on the purpose of life. We consider how best we should live out our relatively short span of existence. We wonder how we should behave towards other people and how we should interact with our environment. These are some of the great issues of existence. They have presumably been raised before recorded history and will presumably continue to be raised for many years into the future.

They are ultimately religious questions and the faiths discussed in this book have tried to respond to them in different ways. We can only marvel at the resolve of human beings through the ages to reflect on these issues and never to abandon the quest of trying to comprehend our place in this universe.

10 THINGS TO REMEMBER

1 *It is possible to have strong religious beliefs while not belonging to an organized religion.*

2 *For some people listening to music or walking in the countryside may be a spiritual experience.*

3 *Some cultures make little distinction between spirituality and life in general.*

4 *Religion may or may not involve the idea of a deity.*

5 *Taoism, while not believing in a single God, has the idea of a spiritual force in the universe.*

6 *On one level Hinduism has many deities, while on a philosophical level it believes in a single universal, spiritual force.*

7 *Some religions involve a sense of withdrawal from the world, while others develop spiritual practice within a worldly context.*

8 *The monastic tradition is found in several faiths.*

9 *In ethical terms some religions are prescriptive, while others set down only general principles for living.*

10 *Prayer, reflection or meditation are important features of spiritual practice.*

2

Confucianism

In this chapter you will learn about:
* *the life and teachings of Confucius*
* *Confucian texts and their teachings*
* *the relationship between Confucianism and Chinese society.*

History

The term 'Confucianism' is derived from the name of Confucius, a Chinese sage, philosopher and teacher, who lived from approximately 551 BCE to 479 BCE. Confucius is actually a Latinized form of the sage's original Chinese name, which was K'ung Fu-tzu. An approximate translation of this would be 'Master K'ung'.

Confucius was born in the area of Lu in China, which now corresponds to the province of Shangdong. It seems likely that he was orphaned fairly early in his life and that his family may not have been sufficiently wealthy to give him access to educational opportunities. However, one can only assume that, at some stage in his early life, Confucius was able either to educate himself or to receive tuition, because he obtained a post in administration and also became a teacher of protocol and formal behaviour. It was very important in Chinese society to appreciate the expected norms of behaviour and discourse in different social situations. Confucius taught his students the conventions of behaviour, which enabled them to move comfortably in different social contexts. It was the norm for these kinds of skill to be acquired only by the higher social classes. They would typically acquire them through the influence of the social milieu in which they mixed and also through formal education. Confucius offered his teaching to people of all social classes and this was somewhat unusual for the China of the time. It suggested something of the philosophy of Confucius in terms of the democratization of knowledge.

There are very few certain details known about the life of Confucius. It is thought that he probably obtained later a fairly senior post in the civil service in Lu and may have held a senior legal post. The teaching of Confucius was perhaps rather less to do with religion in a conventional sense and more about the way in which he felt human beings should behave in day-to-day life and how they should relate to their fellow human beings. He wanted people to be kind towards others and to display a considerate politeness in all their dealings with other people. He hoped that human beings would act sensibly, with careful forethought, and that they would have a sense of their obligations to others. Confucius hoped to persuade the ruler of Lu that these principles were worthwhile and could be incorporated into a system of government. Confucius probably envisaged these principles as being the moral basis of a political system. However, he was unsuccessful in this and those in power in Lu felt unable to adopt his ideals.

Confucius, therefore, felt the need to leave Lu and to attempt to seek out a ruler who would see the merits in his ethical system and would try to implement it. At this time, Confucius had probably reached the age of about 55. For about ten or so years, Confucius seems to have led a fairly itinerant existence as a religious and philosophical teacher, while all the time seeking a sympathetic ruler. He appears not to have found such a person and at about the age of 65 or just over, Confucius travelled back to Lu, where he devoted his final years to expounding his moral system. Confucius did not live long enough to see his theories accepted and put into practice by political leaders. Nevertheless, the democratic approach to educational opportunities espoused by Confucius did have an effect and some time later China developed its renowned system of civil service, one in which entry was based upon ability and open to people of all social classes.

Within only several hundred years after his death, the principles of Confucianism were accepted as the basis of social and political organization in China. These principles were to retain this position for over two millennia.

One of the primary aims of Confucius was to improve the living conditions of the disadvantaged sectors of society. He hoped to achieve this by acting as a catalyst for change in the political system. There was hence a very strong ethical element in his teaching. It was also an ethic which had clear implications for the governance of a state. Confucius sought to start with the established values of China and to reinforce and build on them an approach to life which would go a long way to achieving the political transition which he desired. Such an approach to life was based on a strong sense of consideration towards one's fellow human beings and a devotion to the norms of family life.

The philosophy of Confucius was gradually popularized after his death and other thinkers extended and adapted his thought. Perhaps the leading figure in this respect was Meng-tzu, or Mencius, who lived from approximately 372 BCE to 289 BCE. Mencius was born in a state near Lu in which Confucius was born and like Confucius he was a firm advocate of the virtues of education. He was a believer in the fundamental virtue of human beings, but felt that when people displayed undesirable behaviour it was usually as a result of the unsatisfactory manner in which parents or others had reared them. After Mencius had died, there was a long period during which Buddhism and Taoism became increasingly popular. It seems unlikely that Confucius perceived his philosophy as a religion per se and yet it had some distinctive features of a religion that will be discussed later. Both Buddhism and Taoism presented to people a comprehensive picture of the universe and of the place of human beings within it. This was to some degree lacking in Confucianism and one can understand the consequent appeal of Buddhism and Taoism.

Nevertheless, somewhat later in the Sung dynasty, during the eleventh century, a number of thinkers adapted Confucianism, incorporating within it an increased focus on meditation. The purpose of the meditation was to try to enable adherents to develop the nobler qualities within them and to enable these to be demonstrated in their general behaviour.

This increased concentration on meditation and reflection notwithstanding, Confucianism did not tend to develop the specific types of ritual and worship which characterize many other faiths. This adaptation of Confucianism has sometimes been termed neo-Confucianism. One of the principal philosophers of this movement was called Zhu Xi. He argued that all living or non-living entities are influenced primarily by two factors: there is the *li* or the spiritual energy that pervades and affects the entire universe; and the *ch'i* which is the physical content of each entity. It was particularly important in a spiritual sense for people to try to understand the function of the li, as this had an effect on the entire universe.

Although Confucianism has had an enormous effect upon Chinese thought and way of life, in the twentieth century there was a significant decline in adherence to Confucian principles. It will arguably, however, continue to be embedded in Chinese society in the form of spiritual ethics.

Belief system

Confucianism emerges as a pragmatic response to the world. It seeks to establish a set of strategies for ethical conduct which will help people to adjust in a virtuous way to the situations in which they find themselves. Through this type of moral conduct, the individual then tends to achieve a sense of the spiritual nature of the world.

Confucianism has a number of texts which form the heart of the faith. First of all there are the so-called five classics. Some or all of these may well have been written before the period of Confucius. They comprise the *Book of Changes* (*I Ching*); the *Book of Poetry* (*Shih Ching*); the *Spring and Autumn Annals* (*Ch'un Ch'iu*); the *Book of Documents or History* (*Shu Ching*); and the *Book of Ceremonial* (*Li Chi*). In addition there are the so-called Four Books. These are the *Analects*; the *Doctrine of the Mean*; the *Great Learning* and the *Mencius*.

The *I Ching* may have been written many centuries before the time of Confucius, but he did write an analysis of it. It purports to provide ways of predicting future events. Plant stalks or coins are thrown in order to produce patterns of hexagrams. The book provides a means of understanding the patterns and hence helping people resolve matters about which they are uncertain.

At the heart of Confucianism is a preoccupation with social stability and integration. Confucius placed great emphasis on acting in a humane way. According to him people should reflect their common humanity in all their dealings with other human beings. Humanity could often be demonstrated through the application of behaviour which was considerate and careful in relationships with others. Confucius claimed that if the interactions between people could be conducted in this kind of way, the inevitable result would be a more unified and integrated society. For Confucius, one of the most significant ways in which this integration could be achieved was through reinforcing the role of the family and giving every encouragement to the principle of showing respect for elders and parents.

Insight

Confucianism possesses a strong element of social philosophy. It has religious and psychological elements, but is also deeply concerned about the nature of society, and how society can be organized to care for its members.

One of the central concepts in the moral teaching of Confucius was that of *ren*, a term which can be interpreted and translated in a variety of ways. In one sense ren represents the noblest form of behaviour of which human beings are capable. We might imagine someone in a hazardous situation who sacrifices himself or herself in order to save another. Such a person would be exhibiting ren. A person who is unfailingly generous, even when it disadvantages himself or herself, would be acting with ren.

Insight

There is within the concept of ren a strong sense of ethics; and this morality is related very much to having a sense of responsibility towards other human beings and to the cohesion of society.

Confucius felt that the same quality of ren should be exhibited by political rulers, and the concept formed part of his theory of ethical government. A political leader should, according to Confucius, act always with care and sensitivity towards members of society and they similarly should exhibit a form of ren, by supporting their leader and demonstrating an understanding of the nature of his or her position.

One of the most enigmatic features of Confucianism is whether it can be conceived as a religion or simply as a system of ethical behaviour. Confucius certainly appeared to have a faith which incorporated the concepts of a heaven and also of a divine entity, although the exact nature of the latter was not explained in very precise terms. There was also a faith in the essentially benign and moral nature of the divine. The noble qualities in human beings were rewarded. Moral behaviour was favoured and rewarded by the divine. Confucius also had clear ideas on the nature of religious behaviour. He did not believe that it should include, for example, the use of ritual objects which were supposed to help with divine intervention in human affairs. Although it is rather ambiguous whether Confucius perceived his system as being essentially religious in nature, we can see that there are sufficient such elements within it for it to be reasonably classified it as a religious faith.

Organization

The concept of Confucianism was very much linked to that of the social organization of China. This organization was very structured, from the agricultural level of peasant farmers to the educated administrators of the civil service. Confucianism related to a situation of social cohesion, both in terms of an integration of different types of job role and also in terms of the cohesion of the family and of the political state. Confucianism, however, has not possessed the same degree of hierarchical structure in terms of an organized clergy as in some other faiths. Moreover, it has not possessed the type of religious institutions or the churches and temples with the same kind of functions of ritual, prayer and worship as in some other traditions.

Confucius was also much more of a philosopher and teacher of ethical principles than a religious figure. He did not assume the role of the prophet, neither did he profess to act as an intermediary between God and mankind.

Confucianism, however, although placing great emphasis upon social solidarity, did not encourage an authoritarian structure in society. In fact, although it acknowledged that inevitably people would occupy different social positions in society, it stressed the need for individuals to interrelate with sensitivity and empathy.

Insight

Although there are strong elements of the religious and the spiritual within Confucianism, it is also an approach which places great emphasis upon the nature of the relationship between the individual and the collective society.

Confucianism went as far as specifying five relationships that were regarded as particularly significant in Chinese life and contributed especially to the cohesion of society. These were the relationships between emperor and minister; elder brother and younger brother; father and son; husband and wife; and friend and friend. These relationships were used to illustrate the principles considered to apply between people. The first four of these relationships involved, according to Confucianism, one person with more importance and status than the other. The final relationship, between friends, was not of this nature. Where there was someone with more status, it was important that s/he treated the other person with respect, gave them assistance and advice when necessary and did not use their position to gain any advantage over the other. For their part, the person with less status should respect the position of the other, provide support where necessary and seek to help them in their role. This approach may seem a little different from some social conventions in contemporary European society, but Confucianism arose within the framework of Chinese society at the time. What emerges from this approach is that the ideal type of Confucian relationship was one in which people behaved sensitively and fairly to each other.

Insight

The sense of harmony in life which is a key feature of Confucianism is evident in its approach to relationships. Wherever possible, relationships between people should reflect feelings of empathy for the situation of the other person.

The respect for ancestors and, indeed, their worship has been a long-established element in Confucian practice. Although Confucianism ceased to be the state religion after 1912, the worship of ancestors continued to be widely practised and, indeed, is still practised today. A home may typically have a small shrine dedicated to ancestors. People may also offer prayers to ancestors at a temple.

For Confucius, the ideal way of life was one which exemplified virtuous actions and a sense of harmony with one's surroundings. This feeling of harmony is perhaps illustrated by the practice of Feng Shui, a term which means wind and water. It is a practice which is designed to enable the *ch'i* or energy of the earth to distribute itself evenly and which is characteristically used to determine the position of a proposed building, or to orientate the furniture and other objects within a room. Confucius advocated that human beings should try to live in unity and harmony with their surroundings and through this process they would begin to have an understanding of the spiritual in life.

Insight

The philosophy of living in harmony with the natural world is an approach which tends to be found also in Buddhism and Taoism. Shrines and temples, for example, are often located in positions of natural beauty and tranquillity.

10 THINGS TO REMEMBER

1   *Confucianism is an ethical and spiritual teaching which is derived from the Chinese philosopher Master K'ung, or Confucius.*

2   *It is partly an ethical teaching about how human beings should relate to each other.*

3   *Confucius applied his ethical theories to principles of government.*

4   *Confucian texts became the basis of study for the Chinese civil service.*

5   *Well-known texts include the* I Ching, *the* Analects *and the* Doctrine of the Mean.

6   *Confucius educated people of all social classes.*

7   *He advocated human beings trying to live in harmony with the environment.*

8   *The practice of Feng Shui was derived from this philosophy of harmony.*

9   *Confucianism places great emphasis on the solidarity and cohesion of society.*

10 *Respect for ancestors is an established component of Confucian practice.*

3

Taoism

In this chapter you will learn about:
- *the origins and philosophy of Taoism*
- *Taoism and the natural world*
- *the expression of Taoist principles in art*.

History

Taoism is one of the traditional religions of China. It began as a mystical religious system, but as it became more populist over the centuries, there was a transition to a system involving more ritual centred on local temples. Nevertheless, the fundamental mystical character of the faith has not been extinguished. It seems reasonable to suppose that Taoist ideas have been reflected on for some considerable time, but it is generally claimed that Taoism as a distinct philosophical and religious system may be dated from between the sixth century BCE and the fourth century BCE and owes much to the writings of Lao Tzu and Chuang Tzu.

The central text of Taoism is the *Tao Te Ching*, reputedly written by a sage named Lao Tzu in about the fourth century BCE. Nevertheless, academics have argued about the identity of Lao Tzu and whether, indeed, the name can or should be associated with a single person. The text of the *Tao Te Ching* is composed of often rather brief, succinct sayings and comments, and some people have suggested that it is more likely to be a compilation of the work of several people, rather than that of one person. Another possibility is that the work is derived from philosophical commentaries that were passed on by word of mouth and eventually written down, perhaps by someone named Lao Tzu. Nevertheless, in the absence of definite evidence to the contrary, the *Tao Te Ching* is assumed to have been written by a religious mystic named Lao Tzu, which translates approximately as the Old Master.

A second well-known Taoist work is known as the *Book of Chuang Tzu* and was, by tradition, assumed to have been written by someone of that name. Like the *Tao Te Ching*, this work has a style which suggests it might also be a compilation.

Taoism is fundamentally related to the nature of the *tao*. This is a mystical, spiritual concept which is used in two different but related ways. It is used to describe the spiritual force which pervades the universe and influences everything and everyone within it. Second, it is used to refer to a spiritual discipline or 'way' by which an individual person may understand the nature of the tao and, indeed, become absorbed in it. There are a great number of apparent contradictions in descriptions of the tao, and in some ways these are similar to the issues inherent in writings about other mystical pathways. The tao is claimed to be beyond the understanding of the rational mind and to be comprehended only through experience. In other words, although an individual may follow a path of mystical training and understand the tao, it is regarded as extremely difficult to describe that experience within the framework of logical, scientific language.

Insight

There is an apparent contradiction in that, in order to communicate with another person about the tao, one has to employ language, and yet that very language is an imperfect medium in which to discuss mystical experience.

The original concept of Taoism appears to have been that it was associated with a peaceful, tranquil lifestyle, with people living either in solitude or in a quiet monastic environment. It is also associated with living in a natural setting, in pine forests and mountains, and this is often reflected in Taoist art. Although this tradition continued and has continued to some extent to the present day, by about the first century CE there had developed a tendency for more ritual within Taoism. This was at least partly to meet the needs of those who, while being attracted to Taoism, were not leading the life of a reclusive mystic. The Taoist lifestyle had gradually become, rightly or wrongly, associated with longevity and a lot of attention was given to the development of ritual practices which were supposed to enable people to live longer. This was a deviation in purpose from the original philosophical and spiritual bases of Taoism and yet no doubt resulted in a good deal of popular interest. This trend in Taoism was particularly noticeable from the first to the fourth century CE and is associated with, among others, Chang Ling and, later, Ko Hung.

There were many features in common between Buddhism and Taoism, both in terms of the teaching and in the style of religious practice. They shared, for example, the practice of meditation as a means to spiritual advancement and also the use of breathing exercises as a means to quieten and still the mind. The emphasis on meditation was one factor in the evolution of the school of Buddhist practice known as Ch'an, which later, in a Japanese context, became known as Zen Buddhism. One can see a number of similarities in Taoist and Zen ideas, including for example, the aim of retaining in the mind as few analytic concepts as possible. The purpose of this is to leave the mind free to comprehend, as directly as possible, the nature of reality.

An important concept within Taoism is that of *chih*, or intuitive knowledge. One of the philosophers who discussed this concept was a Taoist who lived in the tenth century CE, called Ssu-ma Cheng-Chen. It was emphasized that chih can only be attained when the individual acquires the ability to let go of the rational, analytic mind and attune himself/herself to inner, intuitive understanding.

Taoism has also inspired a great deal of painting, which has a characteristic and recognizable form. Taoist paintings are typified by the presence of mountains, pine trees, streams and very peaceful settings. They may show a sage sitting by a hut, in the act of meditation; or perhaps someone wandering alone among the mountains. Taoist art is also characterized by the use of empty space. Large areas may be left to the sky or to the space between the mountains. Such space may be thought of as a metaphor for the process of emptying the mind of rational thought. There is also a very characteristic use of ink and paint in such paintings. Often mountains or trees are merely hinted at, using ink washes. Often the artists who painted such pictures spent a great deal of time in meditation themselves and then attempted to reflect their own sense of peace in their art.

Belief system

Taoism is, in its original form, a mystical religion which seeks to enable the individual to comprehend the spiritual force, or tao, which is perceived as the creative influence behind the entire universe.

One of the key concepts of Taoism is *wu-wei*, or non-activity. This is a subtle doctrine which is certainly not the same as advocating lethargy or not making sufficient effort. Perhaps it could be described as being in a state of dynamic equilibrium with the forces in the environment; or it could be thought of in terms of the contemporary adage of relaxing and 'going with the flow'. The paradigmatic instance of this is possibly the natural environment. There is no sense of purpose or of trying to achieve something in nature. Rather, the opposite. Natural events happen in the way that they happen. There is a sense of 'naturalism' about them. Trees shed their leaves in autumn; snow melts in spring; plants flower in summer. There is a normal, natural inevitability about all these events. In fact, these natural events are typical manifestations of the tao. The aim of Taoists is to try to live their lives in a manner whereby they can emulate the 'natural' attitude of nature. The Taoist is not trying to aim towards anything, but rather is allowing life to unfold in whatever way it unfolds. The Taoist is not attempting to acquire or achieve anything. S/he is living in the present, in tune with the developing nature of the world or the tao. It follows that Taoists in their original attitude are little concerned with acquiring material things in the world and, moreover, would probably rather shun such objects. Taoists would probably argue that by relinquishing any notions of acquisition, they do in a sense gain something far more important, which is a peaceful state of mind.

Insight

There is a very subtle balance in the concept of *wu-wei*. It could be perceived as a passive approach to life, and yet this is not the case. It emphasizes a way of acting which is in tune with the natural development of life.

The tao was generally perceived as being immutable and unchanging, but at the same time, there was also the concept of a cyclical process operating in the universe. This cyclical process involved the ideas of *yin* and *yang*. Yin was conceived as an energy formation which was at once passive, and associated with the feminine dimensions of the universe. Yang, by the same token, was seen as a source of energy which was more active than passive, and was also to be related to the masculine features of the world.

The earth was generally associated with the passive elements of the yin, while heaven was normally considered to be more yang-like and active. Yin and yang represented the two opposite polarities of life and existence and out of their combination came such aspects as the sequence of the different seasons. The characteristics of Taoism were a reminder of the yin-like and passive aspects of the universe.

Taoism is not a faith of rigid dogmas and committed beliefs. Rather, it is an approach to life which encourages the individual to try to live in tune with the variations of the natural world. It is perhaps not surprising therefore that Taoists tend to be relativists in terms of ethics. They would thus tend not to espouse a fixed set of ethical principles which they would try to apply to all circumstances. Rather, they would be very flexible in their response to ethical dilemmas, trying to take into account the special circumstances inherent in each situation.

Insight

In contrast with faiths that tend to be rather more prescriptive in ethical terms, Taoism can appear to involve less precise moral values, and yet at the same time its approach is more flexible, allowing the individual to respond to the complexities of each situation.

Traditional Taoist practices usually involved breathing meditation, the purpose of which was to still the mind and make it sufficiently calm for the person to apprehend the tao. This was very similar to the traditional practice of Buddhist meditation where, by concentrating on breathing in and breathing out, the individual is able to calm the mind slowly and reduce the number of spontaneous, extraneous thoughts that enter it. Among ordinary people who were devotees of Taoism, there developed a growing interest in the possibility that the Taoist lifestyle could increase the human lifespan. The possibility fascinated many people and there was an increasing interest in the use of naturally occurring substances which might have medicinal effects on the one hand and perhaps also promote long life on the other. Hence Taoism became associated with such practices and possibilities and a tradition developed of Taoist priests professing expertise in this area. This was not, however, part of the original concept of Taoism, which had a much more purely mystical and meditational orientation.

Another trend in populist Taoism was that there developed a range of deities, which again were not part of the original nature of Taoism. Among the deities are the so-called Jade Emperor and Lao Tzu in a divine form.

Over the centuries there has been a considerable interplay between Taoism, Ch'an Buddhism and Japanese Buddhism. These traditions have all shared the concept of the importance of empty space or the void. The last has, in a metaphorical sense, emphasized the reputed advantages of ridding the mind of rational thought, in order that the individual can experience the tao more directly.

Organization

In terms of everyday practice, Taoism incorporates a range of religious activities, including the use of rituals and festivals, meditation and breathing exercises and the use of slow and disciplined systems of exercise. Individual people will often select a personal deity, who is a person who when living appeared to lead an exemplary life and to provide an example and an inspiration to the present generation. If a Taoist meets a problem in day-to-day life and feels the need for spiritual support, s/he will often pray to a personal deity to seek advice or to receive inspiration on how that deity may have coped with the same situation. Of all the personal deities, people probably most commonly pray to Lao Tzu.

The sense of peace and tranquillity which was an important part of the original Taoism has remained in many aspects of religious practice. The exercises of *tai chi ch'uan* emphasize slow and gradual movements, which are in harmony with the surroundings.

The exercises are conducted in a series of flowing movements and postures and often a great number of different postures are combined together into a long sequence. Such sequences are often combined with breathing exercises. One of the main results of this is a feeling of tranquillity. The mind is calmed by the combination of gentle, non-stressful exercise and the steady breathing. Tai chi is also reputed to have very beneficial effects on the health of practitioners. It is reputed to improve the prospects of living a long life and to improve the condition of the general health. Although tai chi is not a strenuous form of exercise, it nevertheless appears to have a very beneficial effect upon the muscles of the body, apparently reducing the risk of muscle strains. Rather like meditation and yoga, it is also reputed to improve the way in which people interrelate with others, perhaps through making them more relaxed and less prone to tension.

Although tai chi is taught primarily as a form of gentle exercise and as a means of calming and relaxing the mind, it may also be thought of as the basis of some of the Chinese martial arts based upon Taoism. The martial arts related to Taoism have not been developed over the centuries for the purpose of attacking others or of fighting per se, but for defensive purposes. Kung fu is perhaps the best known of such techniques. The 'defensive' martial arts are also generally known for not placing great emphasis on strength and violent techniques. Rather, the practitioner tries to develop a heightened sense of balance and the ability to anticipate the movements and aggression of the opponent. The practitioner then employs this awareness and sensitivity to deflect an attack and to try to use the strength and momentum of the opponent against him or her. Such 'martial' arts are, therefore, not antithetical to the principles of Taoism. They extend the principles of harmony and gentleness into a different type of situation.

The ritualistic ceremonies of Taoism also often try to reflect a sense of empathy with the natural environment. The twin forces of yin and yang are perceived as functioning together harmoniously to create the natural environment of the earth. In addition, the traditional ceremonies and festivals of Taoism are held in parallel to the main events of the agricultural seasons, further emphasizing the relationship between Taoism and the natural world.

The local temple plays an important role in the life of the community, fulfilling many everyday aspects of religious life, including providing help and advice in the case of ill-health and when assistance is required with personal problems. The temples also involve themselves in areas which would be unusual in the West, such as rituals for fortune telling.

Taoism also has a number of rituals that emphasize the cyclical nature of the universe and the importance of the tao within this. Su-ch'i, for example, is a ritual in which symbols of wood, fire, earth, water and metal are embedded in rice plants. This ritual takes place in winter and a prayer is then offered asking for the replenishment of new plants and animals when the warmer weather arrives. It is a ritual which seeks, through the tao, to reinforce the cyclical nature of life. Taoism is thus seen as a faith which emphasizes the natural elements in existence and seeks to encourage people to live in harmony with the tao.

10 THINGS TO REMEMBER

1 *Taoism is a mystical religious system which originated in China.*

2 *The main originator of Taoism is normally reputed to be Lao Tzu.*

3 *The principal text of Taoism is the* Tao Te Ching.

4 *The tao may be thought of as the spiritual force or energy which pervades the universe and affects everything within it.*

5 *The tao is also used to refer to the 'way' or mystical path which should be followed by anyone who wishes to attain union with the tao.*

6 *Taoism is often associated with a tranquil lifestyle and people living in isolated, natural settings.*

7 *Wu-wei, or non-activity, is the art of acting in a practical situation, while at the same time adopting a relaxed approach.*

8 *Yin and yang represent the opposite tendencies in existence; yin is seen as a more passive energy, and yang as a more active energy.*

9 *Taoists tend to attach great importance to the qualities of sensitivity towards one's fellow human beings, moderation in the way in which one lives, and humility in one's attitude to others.*

10 *Taoism is associated with tai chi and the more 'passive' of the 'martial' arts.*

4

....

Shinto

In this chapter you will learn about:
- *the origins of Shinto belief*
- *the relationship between Shinto and Japanese society*
- *the relationship between Shinto and the natural world.*

_____

History

Shinto is the original religion of Japan before the advent of Buddhism. It is not a revealed faith, but appears to have emerged from a complex interaction of devotion to nature, the worship of ancestors and the view that a sense of the spiritual permeates the whole world. Originally this religious perspective was known as *Kami no Michi*, which translates, approximately, as *The Way of the Gods*. Later it became known as Shinto.

This religion does not have a clearly defined set of doctrines. One of its characteristic features is that it entails a profound love and respect for the natural world. Shinto religious shrines are often located in beautiful natural settings and the spiritual entities or gods associated with Shinto are often identified in natural objects such as trees, rocks or rivers. The Japanese word for such spiritual entities is *kami* and they are central to the Shinto system of faith.

> **Insight**
>
> An empathy with nature is an important feature of the
> religious traditions of China and Japan, which are not
> preoccupied exclusively with the philosophical aspects of
> human beings, but with all of the natural world.

The word *kami* is difficult to translate, because they are not really
gods within the Western concept of that term. For believers in
Shinto, there is a spiritual force pervading the universe which
becomes manifest in a number of different entities in the world.
These entities along with their spiritual element are *kami*.
The spiritual entities may be an interestingly shaped rock,
a tree in a particularly beautiful location, or an attractive river.
In this case, a shrine is often built at the location and becomes
the object for veneration or ceremonies. *Kami* may also be a
person, in the sense of perhaps a deceased person who is greatly
admired for the way s/he lived and for his/her achievements.
Kami may also be thought of as revered ancestors, as animals or
as mythological characters.

> **Insight**
>
> An important element of Shinto belief and practice is the
> respect shown to the memory of one's ancestors, and the
> remembrance of them at shrines. The active remembrance of
> ancestors is perhaps more significant in Shinto than in some
> other religions.

Shinto has a very ancient history in Japan, evolving gradually
during the first millennium BCE. When Buddhism arrived in Japan
in the sixth century CE, there was a tendency for a collaborative
relationship in terms of the *kami* of Shinto and the different
forms of the Buddha. On the one hand, adherents of Shinto
tended to regard the Buddha as a form of powerful *kami*,
while, on the other, Buddhists considered *kami* to be different
incarnations of the Buddha. Although there was a degree of
cooperation between the faiths, during the ninth and tenth
centuries CE, there was a tendency for Buddhism to be the
dominant faith.

However, at the beginning of the nineteenth century there was
something of a resurgence of Shinto and in 1867, when the
Japanese emperor assumed full political control, there developed
a much stronger linkage between Shinto and the hierarchy of
the state. Such state Shinto became connected with a range of
ideological beliefs including the divinity of the emperor and the
alleged supremacy of the Japanese people. This type of ideological
perspective derived to some extent from the mythological
connection between the emperor and the most influential *kami*,
Amaterasu, the goddess of the sun. The latter was supposed to
have been the originator of the Japanese race and it was supposed
that the imperial lineage could be traced back to Amaterasu.

At the end of World War II, and after the defeat of the Japanese,
the Americans insisted that the connection between Shinto and the
state of Japan be broken. The emperor was forced to relinquish
his alleged divine status and all jingoistic elements in state Shinto
were eliminated. Shinto has nevertheless continued since the
war, but without its connections to the political hierarchy. Many
Japanese people still visit Shinto shrines and Shinto remains a very
significant element in contemporary Japanese culture.

When Buddhism was first brought to Japan in the sixth century CE,
there were a number of affinities between Shinto and Buddhism.
There was a strong sense of the value of peaceful contemplation
in a natural setting and a respect for the natural world. Neither
religion possessed a monotheistic divinity and both believed in
living and working in the present, valuing the present moment
and the world as it is. The existence of a number of parallels
between the faiths had the result that Japanese people could often
incorporate both Shinto and Buddhist festivals and ceremonies
within their lives, without any sense of conflict between the faiths.

Apart from the traditional and naturalistic aspects of Shinto, there has also been an element of the faith which has been linked to the structural hierarchy of Japanese society. *Kami* were sometimes associated, for example, with some of the traditionally powerful political families. By the nineteenth century, some of the traditional mythologies of early Shinto became associated with the rulers of Japan, giving rise to the strong military philosophy and outlook which became evident in the period leading up to World War II. In this form, Shinto became associated with very strong feelings of support for the Japanese state and for the emperor. After the war, however, Shinto was no longer accepted as the religion of the Japanese state. It could be argued that the militaristic associations of Shinto at this period were not at all typical of the original nature of the faith, with its emphasis on living in a state of equilibrium with the natural world.

Belief system

There is a strongly pragmatic element in Shinto, which is derived from a perception of the world as being the principal reality in a philosophical sense. Some religions have a strongly mystical element that involves the assumption that there is another, spiritual world which is in a sense superior to the physical world and with which it is desirable to make contact and to merge one's spirit or soul. This is not a strongly held concept in Shinto. This present world is perceived as being the principal reality and the one with which all human beings must come to terms, with which they must relate. It follows from this perspective that there is not the same type of ascetic tradition in Shinto as exists in some other faiths. Indeed, far from rejecting the world as it is, Shinto seeks to celebrate the world. Hard work, success and the attainment of considerable wealth are not seen as being in any way antithetical to the spiritual life. There is a naturalness about Shinto which seeks to emphasize the religious in the normal, everyday way of conducting one's existence. In fact, it is perhaps of note that originally in Japan, there was a time when religion and spirituality were not given a specific, individual name such as Shinto. Spirituality was simply a part of life. It was only with the advent of Buddhism that a means was required of distinguishing between the indigenous faith and the incoming religion. It was only then that a name was given to the indigenous religion, providing an opportunity, if required, to distinguish it from the activities of everyday life.

The value system of Shinto consists fundamentally of the values of the natural, unspoilt world. These are the values of purity, lack of affectation, lack of ostentation and the aesthetics of nature. Cleanliness and bathing are particularly esteemed and regarded as an important part of Japanese tradition. Nevertheless, definitions of what should count as moral and ethical behaviour have not been traditionally associated with Shinto. In this sense, the definition of the ethical rests on rational analysis of the issues involved, rather than on compliance with a set of religious principles.

Although Shinto believes in the existence of a spiritual force that pervades the universe, there also exists a strong mythology of deities within Shinto. The early mythological tales associated with Shinto relate the union between Izanagi-no-mikoto and Izanami-no-mikoto which resulted in the creation of Japan. The *Ko ji Ki* and the *Nihon Shoki*, two of the principal scriptural texts associated with Shinto written early in the eighth century CE, reflect this mythological tradition. Amaterasu, the goddess of the sun, has a famous shrine at Ise. She is generally regarded as the most important *kami*. Inari is the deity of rice, while Hachiman is the god of warfare. Tenjin is the deity associated with education. There are many shrines to the deities and also to other *kami*. They may be simple roadside shrines or large shrines in the major cities. However, the typical features of a Shinto shrine are that it is simple in design and located in a place of natural beauty.

Insight

The wide distribution of Shinto shrines, both large and small, ensures among other things that the religion is very much an element of everyday life, rather than something separated from daily existence.

Although there is an acceptance in Shinto of the importance of the peaceful, contemplative aspects of life, existence is also acknowledged to incorporate more violent and uncontrolled elements. Shinto acknowledges the opposite polarities in the human soul of peace and tranquillity on the one hand and upheaval of emotions on the other.

Organization

Kami are worshipped at communal shrines or at small shrines in the family home. People may ask the *kami* for help in time of illness or for advice if they are faced with a personal problem. Shrines are very common in Japan and are often marked by an entrance called a *torii*. This consists of two upright posts and two cross-pieces at the top. The posts and cross-pieces may be made of wood or stone. The principal significance of the *torii* is that it separates the secular surroundings of the shrine from the spiritual area within.

Upon entering the shrine, there is a fairly standard, conventional way for the devotee to behave. At the entrance to the shrine there is usually a container of clean water and some scoops or ladles. The devotee uses the water to wash the mouth and hands ritually before beginning to pray. It is usual next to make some offerings to the *kami* of the shrine. In a public shrine the offering will most likely involve a donation of money. At a family shrine, it may simply be a small quantity of food. The visitor next bows solemnly twice; claps the hands twice; and then bows again.

The purpose of visiting the shrine may be simply to pray or to make offerings. Very often, however, people visit a shrine in order to ask for assistance from the *kami*. A person starting a new enterprise such as a business may ask for support with this, while a student about to undertake examinations may visit a shrine in order to ask for help. Shrines are also an important focus for the key rites of passage in life. Several weeks after a birth, the baby will be taken to the shrine. From that point onwards the assumption is that the baby is being protected by the *kami* of the shrine. Weddings are also typically associated with Shinto shrines. It is perhaps significant that death is regarded as impure within the Shinto philosophy of life and rites after death are usually performed at a Buddhist shrine rather than a Shinto shrine. This is perhaps a good example of the relationship between the two faiths and the way in which they complement one another.

Insight

Shinto shrines are very important places of pilgrimage, with people sometimes travelling long distances to visit notable shrines, or those located in places of natural beauty.

Shrines are also a place where the future is foretold. Often at shrines you will see predictions written on pieces of paper which are tied on strings to the branches of trees. When people visit the shrine they pay a small amount and take away one of these predictions. Visitors may go to the shrine with hand-written requests for help from the *kami*. These will be left at the shrine in the hope that the *kami* will respond.

Purity is very important in Shinto. This is reflected in the washing before entry to the shrine and also in the natural settings of many shrines. Visitors also often take flowers to shrines as an offering.

Shrines may be very small, such as those found at the roadside, but may also be more substantial. At the larger shrines there may be a variety of buildings. There may be a house for the priest and also a place where visitors may purchase small devotional objects. It is not usual to visit a shrine if a person is unwell, as this is considered ritually impure.

10 THINGS TO REMEMBER

1 *Shinto is the original, indigenous religion of Japan.*

2 *Shinto means 'The Way of the Gods'.*

3 *The two faiths of Shinto and Buddhism have tended to coexist harmoniously.*

4 *Shinto involves a complex interaction between devotion to nature, worship of ancestors and belief in spiritual elements in both people and the natural world.*

5 *Shinto believes in the idea of a spirit which permeates the universe and which shows itself as individual* kami.

6 Kami *or 'spirits' are believed to be present in natural objects, people and mythological characters.*

7 *The most significant* kami *is Amaterasu, the goddess of the sun.*

8 Kami *are worshipped at shrines.*

9 *Shrines are often located in places of great natural beauty, such as among trees or by a river.*

10 *Purity and cleanliness are strong elements in the Shinto way of life.*

5

....

Judaism

In this chapter you will learn about:
- *the origins and belief system of Judaism*
- *the key texts of Judaic belief*
- *the religious customs of Judaism.*

_____

History

It is to some extent a matter of judgement where one places the
origin of Judaism in history, but it is not unreasonable to begin
with Abraham. He came originally from the city of Ur, on the
river Euphrates. This area is located in what is now southern Iraq.
About 2,000 years BCE, Ur was subject to invasion and it was this
factor that probably caused Abraham to lead the Hebrew tribes
away towards fresh territories. He left, accompanied by his wife
Sarah, and travelled first northwards to Haran and then back
south to Canaan, which was located approximately in the area of
contemporary Israel. Canaan was the so-called 'Promised Land'.
It was so promised in an agreement between Abraham and the
single God that he worshipped. In this covenant, God promised
that Canaan would belong to Abraham and his tribe.

At some point in approximately the eighteenth or seventeenth
century BCE, poor harvests in Canaan caused many of the Hebrews
to move southwards and live on the northern borders of Egypt,

where food was more plentiful. At first the Egyptians and Hebrews lived harmoniously in close proximity, but there came a time when one of the Egyptian pharaohs began to view the Hebrews as a potential source of forced labour and they became slaves to the Egyptians, being compelled to work particularly on the construction of new buildings.

As the population of the Israelites increased, however, the Egyptians became concerned that there might be an insurrection and the pharaoh decided on the cruel and drastic measure of ordering the killing of every young Israelite boy. The child Moses was born at this unfortunate period and his mother, naturally fearing for his safety, hid him in bulrushes. The pharaoh's daughter found him, however, and arranged for him to be taken back to the pharaoh's palace where Moses grew up as a member of the Egyptian aristocracy. Although he did not experience the suffering of the Israelites, he must have seen many examples of that suffering. One day, when an Egyptian was intent on attacking an Israelite, Moses intervened and killed the Egyptian. As a result of this action, he left Egypt and lived in Midian. It was at this stage of his life that Moses had a communication from God through the medium of the burning bush and felt a mission to lead the Israelites out of slavery in Egypt to the promised land of Canaan. The pharaoh, however, had no incentive to release the Israelites, and intended to keep them as slaves. Subsequently, a series of plagues afflicted Egypt, and the pharaoh, connecting the incidence of these disasters with the policy of keeping the Israelites, decided to release them. Having been held in slavery for over 400 years, the Israelites set off on the long trek back to Canaan, in an event which has become known as the Exodus.

Once they had left, however, the pharaoh had a change of heart and sent soldiers to recapture the Israelites. The soldiers in their chariots made up ground on the Israelites and had almost caught them by the time they had reached the so-called Red Sea. The Israelites managed to pass across safely, while many of the following Egyptians were drowned. A possible rational explanation of this event, which enabled the Israelites to escape, was that the area of water in question was heavily overgrown with reeds and water plants. This was sufficient to enable the Israelites to walk quickly across, while the heavy chariots of the Egyptians weighed down the reeds, causing many of the soldiers to drown. Whatever the explanation, the Israelites made good their escape and wandered on into the desert.

Eventually, the great caravan of people reached Mount Sinai and Moses set off up the mountain in order to pray and commune with God, or *Yahweh*. Moses was commanded by God to tell the Israelites that they should not construct any images of other divinities out of gold or silver. God gave Moses two stone tablets inscribed with the rules of conduct for the Israelites including the Ten Commandments. These tablets were to be kept in the Ark of the Covenant, which was to be constructed from acacia wood and gold, according to instructions given to Moses by God. God also instructed Moses that the Israelites should maintain the Sabbath as a day free from work. However, as Moses descended from Mount Sinai, he realized that the Israelites had, in his absence, constructed a religious image of a gold bull calf. One of the responses of Moses was to break the two stone tablets which he had carried down the mountain. However, these tablets were ultimately replaced.

Eventually, the Israelites reached the border of the promised land of Canaan. God told Moses to climb Mount Nebo and look out across the expanse of Canaan. It was here that Moses died. He had declared that he wished Joshua to be his successor and it was Joshua who now led the Israelites in their conquest of the peoples who lived in Canaan.

By the period of the eleventh century BCE, a single king ruled over Israel. Saul was the son of Kish, who was a member of the tribe of Benjamin. Samuel anointed Saul, according to the command of God, as the King of all Israel. The biblical account portrays this period as one of great intertribal warfare, which took place over a relatively small geographical area. One may only conclude that life must have been extremely uncertain and insecure for the ordinary citizens of this time. Certainly, for the duration of the reign of Saul, there was an almost continuous state of war between Philistia and Israel. Saul was an extremely successful general, overcoming the army which besieged Jabesh and defeating the armies of Moab, Ammon and Edom. Saul's son Jonathan also killed the Philistine general in authority in Geba.

The biblical account suggests that Saul fell out of favour with God and that Samuel was guided by God to anoint David, the son of Jesse of Bethlehem, as the future King of Israel. Apparently as something of a coincidence, David came to the attention of Saul and the latter appointed him to his staff, giving him the job of carrying his armaments. As David became a member of Saul's court, he met Saul's son Jonathan, and they became the very closest of friends. When David, in the famous episode, killed Goliath of Gath in single combat, David became understandably very popular with the soldiers and ordinary people. He was hailed as a hero and Saul became unnecessarily jealous. David was quickly making a reputation for himself as a great soldier and leader of men and this further disconcerted Saul. It was at about this period that David married Michal, Saul's daughter. It appears that Saul possibly allowed some of these rather negative emotions to affect him and to make him less well adjusted towards the world. The end came on Mount Gilboa in a fierce battle against the Philistines, when the latter got much the better of the conflict. Saul suffered serious wounds and realizing that he would not escape, decided to fall on his own sword. Three of his sons, including Jonathan, also lost their lives in the battle.

David was initially anointed King of Judah and he reigned as such from Hebron for over seven years. After this period, representatives of the different tribes of Israel travelled to Hebron to pay their respects to David and to appoint him King of Israel, in addition to his ruling over Judah. David moved the seat of his government to Jerusalem and from there he ruled over Israel and Judah for over 30 years. One of David's sons, by his wife Bathsheba, was named Solomon and it was he whom David selected to succeed him as the King of both Israel and Judah. Solomon extended the boundaries of the land ruled by David and ultimately his influence stretched from the river Euphrates to Egypt and to Philistia.

Under Solomon the country prospered and he initiated a large-scale programme of construction, particularly the building of a temple at Jerusalem and a palace for himself. These projects took an enormous amount of labour and Solomon used the members of the original tribes which had inhabited Canaan as labour. These people included Hittites, Jebusites and Amorites. According to the account in the Bible, Solomon employed 30,000 men cutting and transporting cedar and pine logs, and 80,000 men cutting and trimming the stone for the temple in Jerusalem. It seems that the labourers in the quarry knew the required shape for all the stones, since the stone was cut exactly to shape at the quarry in order to avoid making any noise during the actual building process. Building work commenced on the temple 480 years after the Exodus from Egypt. In the construction of the temple, cedar beams were used for all the supporting work and many of the walls inside were lined with cedar panels. At the rear of the temple, the Holiest Place was built to contain the Covenant Box. The latter was the repository for the two stone tablets which Moses had held at Mount Sinai during the trek from Egypt to the Promised Land. Gold was liberally used to decorate the inside of the temple. In addition to the temple, Solomon built his own palace, the construction of which took 13 years.

When Solomon died after a reign of 40 years, Jeroboam became King of the ten northern tribes of Israel, while Rehoboam became leader of the two remaining tribes of Judah and Benjamin, in the southern kingdom of Judah. Unfortunately for Israel, however, great armies were on the move. In 722 BCE, King Shalmaneser of Assyria, and later his successor Sargon II, surrounded the city of Samaria in Israel and laid siege to it. Assyria was one of the great powers of the time, with its capital at Nineveh, which was near the city of Mosul in modern Iraq. The siege lasted approximately three years and the Assyrians were victorious. They transported many people from the ten tribes back to Assyria and, in their place, in order to consolidate their hold over Israel, a number of people from Assyria became settlers in the Samaritan towns. Eight years later, Sennacherib, the then ruler of Assyria, attacked the southern lands of Judah.

By 586 BCE, the Babylonians became dominant and King Nebuchadnezzar laid siege to Jerusalem while Jehoiachin was the King of Judah. Eventually, Jerusalem had to surrender to a superior force and the city was raided, with the gold and art works of the Temple and palace being removed and transported to Babylon, a city on the lower Euphrates in what is now Iraq. Nebuchadnezzar viewed the people of Judah as a resource, making sure that he took back to Babylon all the trained and skilled people, including carpenters, builders, goldsmiths and other artisans. This transportation of the people of Judah became known by the term diaspora, which means approximately 'dispersal'.

By 539 BCE, however, the Babylonians were defeated by the armies of King Cyrus of Persia. Cyrus gave the Jewish captives their freedom and allowed them to return to their homeland. Indeed, he encouraged them to return home and to rebuild the temple at Jerusalem. Not all the Jews returned, but many of those who did went to live in Jerusalem and began the process of accumulating building materials for the new temple. Cedar logs were again purchased from Lebanon and by 516 BCE, the new temple was nearly finished. Many Jews, however, did not leave Babylonia, choosing to remain there and sustain their culture and religion in that context. To some extent the Jews had been successful in maintaining their way of life in a different country and had been allowed to continue their religious practices by both the Babylonians and the Persians. Some Jews were appointed to positions of considerable authority in the society, and gained a degree of political power.

A subsequent Persian king, Artaxerxes, had sufficient faith in one of the Hebrew prophets, Ezra, to grant him a specific dispensation to return to Jerusalem and to begin the process of renewing and reforming the Judaic faith. Ezra returned in 458 BCE and then in 446 BCE Nehemiah was despatched in order to assume the role of governor of Judea. He and Ezra joined forces and worked together towards the goal of religious renewal. Ezra attempted to emphasize the function of the Torah in defining a common heritage for the Jewish people, and in trying to provide a basis for uniform belief throughout the peoples of the diaspora, whether they be located in Egypt, Babylon or elsewhere. The Torah consists of the first five books of the Bible. The word 'torah' may mean both 'teaching' and 'law'.

Further major political and social changes took place in 333 BCE when Alexander the Great conquered Israel and Babylonia. Generally speaking, Alexander was tolerant towards the Jewish people and allowed them to continue in sustaining their own religion. There was, however, a gradual process of Hellenization taking place, initiated by Alexander and which continued after his death in 323 BCE with the dynasty of the Ptolemies.

When the latter gained control over Palestine and Egypt, one of the consequences of the advance of Greek culture was that many Jews started to lose the skill of reading and speaking Hebrew and assumed the use of Greek. The *Pentateuch* was thus translated into Greek. The Greek translation of the entire Bible was called the *Septuagint*. In 198 BCE the process of Greek influence continued with the Seleucid dynasty seizing power in Palestine.

By approximately the middle of the second century BCE, there were some Jews who believed that it would be a pragmatic measure to incorporate Judea within the empire created by Greece and Syria. Others, however, felt that such a measure would be a betrayal of the Jewish religion and cause. Matters were, to some extent, brought to a head when the emperor Antiochus declared that there should be an end to Jewish religious customs. This caused considerable antagonism in some quarters and there were demonstrations and the outbreak of violence, demanding a return to the principles of the Torah. Fighting broke out between the Jews who supported Jewish autonomy and Syrian soldiers. Judas Maccabeus was the principal leader of the rebels. He inflicted a number of defeats on the Syrians and managed to recapture Jerusalem in 165 BCE. Following the death of Antiochus in

163 BCE there was a reduction in the level of conflict and a measure of autonomy for the Jews resulted.

The Romans began to exert more and more influence and in 63 BCE Pompey's army secured Judea, transforming it into a province of Rome. In 39 BCE Herod was appointed King of Judea by the Romans. He was the son of Antipater, the Procurator of Judea. It appears that, under the Romans, many restrictions were placed on the Jews. In 66 CE the so-called Zealots rebelled against the Roman rulers and, in response, Titus laid siege to and then destroyed Jerusalem. There were subsequent persecutions and circumstances did not relax for the Jews until Antoninus became emperor. By that time many Jews had left Judea to join others in the diaspora. It is worth mentioning two important groupings among the Jews. The Pharisees numbered many scribes and rabbis among their members and as a party were very much preoccupied with religious issues. They were very much concerned to maintain the requirements of the Law and the traditions and precepts of Judaism. The Sadducees, in contrast, although also committed to maintaining religious traditions, had more of an interest in the exercise of political power than did the Pharisees. While the Romans were in power in the region, however, they were only able to engage in political action to a minimal extent.

The conversion of the Roman Emperor Constantine to Christianity in the fourth century CE and the adoption of Christianity as the official religion of the Roman Empire created a certain amount of further pressure upon Judaism. The *Talmud* became of increasing importance in providing a unifying influence for the various scattered Jewish communities, particularly in the light of the declining influence of the historical centres of study and learning in Babylon and in Jerusalem. The Talmud consists of rabbinical commentaries and analyses of Jewish law and religion.

After Christianity, the next major historical influence was that of Islam. Muslim armies were victorious in Iraq in the seventh century, yet the Jewish communities in that part of the world appeared to live in relative harmony under, for example, the

Abbasid caliphate. For some time, Spain was a leading centre of Jewish culture, but periodic conflict and persecutions led to a Jewish emigration from Spain. A key figure of the Jewish culture in Spain was the philosopher Moses Maimonides. In medieval times in Europe, persecutions of the Jewish communities took place periodically and were at times horrifically violent. The scattered communities of the diaspora naturally looked back to the country of their origins and Theodore Herzl, who was born in 1860 CE, led the movement for a Jewish state in Palestine. This so-called Zionist movement held its first Congress in Basel in Switzerland in 1897. The migration of Jews to Palestine was supported to some extent by the Balfour Declaration of 1917, which gave conditional support for a Palestinian Jewish homeland.

In 1933 a chain of events started that was to lead to the Holocaust, an event of almost unbelievable inhumanity. On the assumption of power by Adolph Hitler in Germany, anyone with a Jewish grandparent was defined as belonging to the Jewish race and hence became a legitimate target for increasingly violent persecution and ultimately extermination. On *Kristallnacht* in 1938 synagogues were destroyed and then in 1941 the decision was taken by the Nazis to implement the *Endlösung* or 'Final Solution' as it was called. Extermination camps were constructed and approximately six million European Jews died in gas chambers. This amounted to the physical extermination of about two-thirds of the Jewish population of Europe. Ultimately, the work of the Zionist movement came to fruition and the state of Israel came into existence in 1948.

Belief system

The principal religious texts of Judaism include the Torah and the Talmud. The Torah contains the books of Genesis, Exodus, Leviticus, Numbers and Deuteronomy, the first five books of the Bible. The Hebrew Old Testament was defined in terms of its content by the Council of Jamnia, convened in 90 CE. The word 'torah' comes from the Hebrew term signifying 'instruction', 'teaching' or 'law'.

The Talmud consists of comments, analyses and discussions on a variety of subjects related to Judaism, but particularly there are writings connected with Jewish law or *halakhah*. The commentaries are written by rabbis, from about the period of Ezra to approximately the fifth century CE. The language of the Talmud is a combination of Hebrew and Aramaic. There are in fact two Talmuds, one written in Babylon and the other in Jerusalem. The Babylonian Talmud is by far the longer, in fact, about three times as long. The fundamental concern of the Talmud is the way in which human beings can relate to God. Moreover, the Talmud is intended to be very practical in nature, rather than being devoted to abstract theological discussion. The contributors to the Talmud tried to analyse practical everyday problems, and founded that analysis on the scriptures.

Insight

One sees in the Talmud, among other writings, the long tradition of scholarship within Judaism, and the importance attached to study and to reflection upon religious themes.

The rabbis of the Talmud employed techniques such as parables to try to convey some of the religious principles of the Bible. Theologically speaking, Judaism asserts that there is only one God and that Jews worship this God. Judaism affirms that one ought to believe in this monotheistic God and try to act in accordance with the wishes of God. Jews regard God as omniscient and hence feel that he can look into the hearts and minds of human beings, and interpret their thoughts and actions. The Talmud lays great stress on an ethical way of behaving in life. It provides guidance and instruction to cater for a wide range of contexts in which human beings might find themselves. Jews are expected to display high ethical standards in their business and commercial dealings. Wealth and financial prosperity are not regarded as necessarily undesirable and there is not in Judaism the strong trend towards asceticism which one may find in some other religions. Indeed, the acquisition of wealth is sometimes regarded as a concomitant of a life devoted to God.

Insight

There is an apparent contrast between Judaism (and religions related to it) and the traditions which have developed in the Indian subcontinent. The former tend to be generally more prescriptive, for example in ethics and questions of belief, than the latter.

Jews are especially urged to be sensitive to the position of strangers and foreigners in their midst, to treat them fairly and with consideration and not to indicate any ways in which they might be different from the indigenous or majority people. Great emphasis is placed on the virtue of human liberty and free will. Although Jews are to some extent constrained by religious customs and conventions, there is also a sense within Judaism that freedom and independence of thought are important aspects of life. Jews are also encouraged to care for those who are less fortunate and who have insufficient to eat. They are exhorted to engage in charitable giving and to treat others in the same manner in which they would wish to be treated.

Arguably the central element of the Jewish faith is that the world is the creation of God. There is also a sense of teleology in the faith, in that the universe is seen as moving towards a particular goal and that God is believed to be directing the universe with certain aims in mind. It is also believed that God influences each human being through the human soul, the qualities of which are derived ultimately from God. In the biblical account, God also regards the Jews as a people who are special in His eyes and it is part of the covenant or agreement reached between God and the descendents of Abraham that the Jewish people would inherit the land of Canaan.

There is also a mystical tradition within Judaism which is known as the *Kabbalah*. Indeed, the word actually means 'tradition'.

The Kabbalah is a process of spiritual training which enables human beings to gain access to, and to unite themselves with, spiritual forces which have existed within the Jewish tradition for many years. Adherents of the Kabbalah claim that one of its functions is to counteract negative influences in the world and to help to reinforce the position of religion in the world. It is suggested that there are mystical tendencies in the Bible, particularly in relation to the visions experienced by the prophets. As in the mystical traditions of other religions, the Kabbalah emphasizes the practice of meditation, although there are not the same type of ascetic practices that one finds in religions such as Hinduism. One of the principal religious texts of the Kabbalah is the *Zohar*, which is an analysis and discussion of the Torah. The Kabbalah also stresses that adherents should seek to develop a strong sense of love for their fellow human beings, as a very important component of the mystical, spiritual quest.

Insight

The Kabbalah is in many ways a complex and esoteric tradition. There is a long tradition of philosophers producing reflections upon the mystical quest, and observations about how human beings can develop a closer relationship with God.

The mystical tradition of Kabbalah has three main elements. The aspirant first tries to develop an understanding of the nature of the divine, then strives to develop a love of God, and finally works to be able to communicate directly with God. These spiritual abilities are typically seen as being conveyed by the teachings of a spiritual guide. Within Judaism, the tradition of mysticism is closely interwoven with everyday religious life, and is seen rather less as a separate esoteric practice. In this respect Kabbalah is perhaps slightly different to mystical approaches in other faiths.

Over the centuries, a large body of writing associated with Kabbalah has developed. Some of it is very theoretical, including conjectures for coming to terms with the nature of human existence. There are many writings which have a strong astrological tendency, whose purpose is to provide people with strategies for understanding the world and its phenomena. Finally, there are writings which describe mystical processes through which aspirants can attempt to gain a direct appreciation of God. There have been many celebrated practitioners of Kabbalah over the centuries, but two leading historical figures were Abraham Abulafia (1240–92) and Isaac Luria (1534–72).

Prayer is an extremely important activity in the Jewish faith. There are a number of prayers in Judaism which have been used for many years; but of all prayers, perhaps the *Shema* is the most significant. It affirms the basic beliefs of Judaism, that there is a single God and that all Jews should devote themselves to the love of God.

Insight

Monotheism as a religious philosophy permeates Judaism, with most aspects of religious practice being oriented towards the idea of a single, omnipotent God, who cares for those who are devoted to Him.

In the synagogue, there are a number of objects and customs which are associated with prayer. Men usually wear the skull cap or *yarmulkah*. This is normal for orthodox Jews, but reform Jews do not typically wear it. In orthodox synagogues, men wear the prayer robe or *tallit* around themselves during the act of prayer. Women as well as men wear the tallit in reform synagogues. Men also traditionally wear the *tefillin* during prayer. These are leather boxes linked to leather straps, which are worn on the front of the head and on the arm while praying. The boxes contain extracts from the scriptures.

Organization

Within Judaism, the synagogue is the location for communal worship, although it should be noted that much that is central to the Judaic religious life also takes place in the home. The word 'synagogue' signifies 'meeting' and this indicates something of the communal function. Originally, the place of worship associated with Judaism had been the Temple at Jerusalem, but the practice of creating a number of different places of worship possibly developed at some time during the period when Jews were held captive in Babylonia. In contemporary times, synagogues may exist in several different forms and designs. At the entrance to the synagogue one often finds the *mezuzah*. This is a decorative container holding a scroll with the prayer, the Shema, written on it. The mezuzah is usually fixed to the architrave of the front door of the synagogue.

There are a number of differences in the pattern of worship and customs of an orthodox synagogue, compared with those of a reform synagogue. In the orthodox synagogue men officiate during the service and the women and men sit separately. In the reform synagogue, however, women may take a full part in the religious ceremonies.

Perhaps the part of the synagogue with the most religious significance is the Holy Ark. This symbolizes the Ark of the Covenant, which was the container in which Moses placed the tablets inscribed with the Ten Commandments after he had descended from Mount Sinai. In a synagogue, the Ark may consist of an enclosed cabinet to hold the scrolls on which are written the Torah, or first five books of the Bible. The scrolls are often written by hand. The Ark is normally constructed on the side of the synagogue which faces towards Jerusalem and it is in this direction that people face during prayer and worship. The Ark may be enclosed with velvet curtains which are ornately decorated and sometimes the scrolls inside are placed within outer covers which are highly decorated. Usually a lamp or light is kept burning over the Ark all the time, and this replicates a light that was traditionally maintained over the holiest place in the temple at Jerusalem. In addition, fixed above the Ark, are usually copies of the two stone tablets that were held by Moses at Mount Sinai and which have engraved on them part of the Ten Commandments.

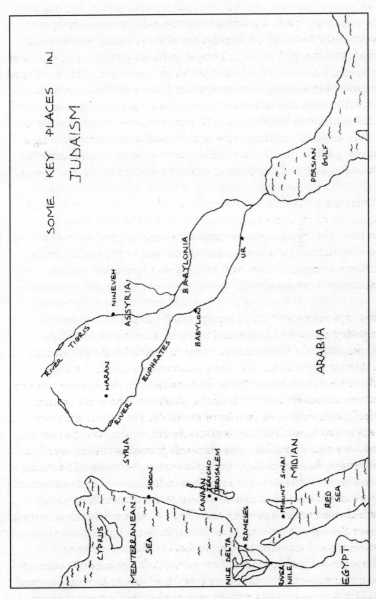

Figure 5.1 Some key places in Judaism.

In a central position in the synagogue, there is an elevated platform to which the Torah is taken during religious services and from which it is read to the congregation. The platform is known as the *bimah*.

In orthodox Judaism, the maintenance of the Sabbath (from Friday sunset to Saturday sunset) is regarded as extremely important. On Friday evenings both men and young men go to the synagogue to attend prayers. On the morning of the Sabbath, the family attends the synagogue, but it is normally only the men who participate in the main religious activities. The women and girls often sit in a gallery built around the top of the synagogue and do not take part in the main religious service.

In the Hebrew language, the Sabbath is known as *Shabbat*. For Jews, the Sabbath is probably the most significant of the remembrances of the faith and it is also worth noting that the Sabbath is identified in the Ten Commandments as a day to be remembered separately. It is a very important day to Jews for forgetting the matters of the rest of the week and concentrating on the spiritual. This function is reflected in the Hebrew linguistic origins of the word Shabbat, as *shin-bet-tav*, which means to finish doing something or to rest.

One of the most important functions of the Sabbath is to encourage Jews to remember the reasons for keeping the day holy. The Sabbath is, first, an occasion on which to remember and reflect upon the creation of the world. In the book of Genesis it is recorded that God made the heavens and earth and then rested on the seventh day. By remembering the Sabbath, Jews are also remembering and thinking about the role of God in the act of creation and in bringing about the world in which they live. In addition, in the book of Deuteronomy, Moses reminds the Jews that remembering the Sabbath is also associated with their servitude in Egypt and the role of God in assisting their escape. Thus the Sabbath has not only a function in helping Jews to remember significant religious events, but also a practical function in declaring a day of rest and renewal after the work of the week and giving people time to reflect on their lives in general and the spiritual elements therein. The remembrance of creation and of the escape from Egypt are both components of the *kiddush* prayer which is said on Friday evenings. The other important element of the Sabbath is that certain types of work are forbidden on that day.

The observance of the Sabbath tends to follow a fairly traditional sequence. On Friday afternoon as many jobs as possible are done to prepare for the Sabbath, particularly those activities which are prohibited on this day. A lot of cooking is usually done to ensure that sufficient food is prepared for the entire Sabbath.

Insight

The migration of Jewish communities around the world, often sadly because of persecution, has resulted in the spread of Jewish culture, so that many aspects of the latter, including for example Jewish cuisine, have become well known.

Sabbath begins at sunset on Friday evening. In the home special candles are lit, and just before sunset Sabbath prayers are said and the family typically goes to the synagogue for a service. After this, the family returns home and the father says the kiddush prayer. Afterwards a prayer is said over some special loaves of bread called *challah*. There is then the Friday evening Sabbath meal and, on its completion, a prayer called *birkat hamazon* is said. On the Saturday morning, most of the time is devoted to services at the synagogue, which are followed by another Sabbath meal at home. The afternoon is devoted to a period of rest, discussion and study of the scriptures. There might be another short meal before darkness comes, marking the end of the Sabbath.

In the communities attached to reform synagogues, there is generally a slightly more relaxed approach to the Sabbath customs. In reform synagogues, prayers are often said in the local language rather than in Hebrew. Also, reform Jews do not tend to attach such complete authority to the Torah, regarding it as the unchanging will of God; they rather see it as reflecting the evolving and developing relationship between God and the Jewish people.

There are a large number of religious festivals which are associated with Judaism. There is the *Bar Mitzvah* celebration, a form of rite of passage for young men. It is a celebration which marks the transition from childhood to adulthood, and is traditionally held shortly after a boy's 13th birthday. The significance of the ceremony is that afterwards the boy is regarded as a man, particularly in the sense of acknowledging responsibility for his own actions and trying to behave in the spirit of Judaism. In reform synagogues, there is a similar festival for girls, the *Bat Mitzvah*, which has the same purpose, marking their passage into full adulthood.

Other festivals have a strong sense of history and of remembering historical events for the Jewish people. The festival of *Yom Kippur* is a day on which Jews make a special attempt to remember their God. It is a remembrance of the occasion when Moses descended from Mount Sinai with the stone tablets on which were inscribed the Ten Commandments. Yom Kippur is largely a day when Jews fast and pray to God that they may be forgiven their wrong deeds.

Yom Kippur is the 'Day of Atonement' and its basic function is to enable people to think back over the past year and then to ask God for forgiveness for the things they have done wrong. It is a very widely observed day in the Jewish community. Yom Kippur is normally a day of complete fasting, from before sunset on one evening to after darkness on the following day. Most of the actual day of Yom Kippur is devoted to prayer and services at the synagogue.

Perhaps the best-known of Jewish festivals is Passover, or *Pesach*, which celebrates the events leading up to the escape of the Israelite people from Egypt. As described in Exodus 11–13, the Egyptian pharaoh would not release the Israelites from slavery and, ultimately, the God of the Israelites said that He would kill each firstborn among the Egyptians. The Israelites were told to mark their doors with the blood of a dead animal, so that during the night the Lord would know to 'pass over' the homes of the Israelites, but kill the firstborn in each Egyptian house. This indeed happened and the pharaoh was so distraught by this event that he told the Israelites to leave at once. They did not have time to leaven their bread with yeast, so speedy was their departure, and took with them only unleavened dough. This explains the significance to this day of Jewish homes not having any leavened bread within them at the time of Passover. The Israelites had been held under conditions of slavery for about 430 years, were finally released, escaped the pursuit of the Egyptians and, ultimately, settled in the promised land of Canaan.

10 THINGS TO REMEMBER

1 *The mystical tradition in Judaism is known as the Kabbalah.*

2 *The festival of Yom Kippur is a day of atonement for sins.*

3 *The Bar Mitzvah for boys and the Bat Mitzvah for girls are rites of passage indicating the transition to adulthood.*

4 *The festival of Pesach, or Passover, acts as a remembrance of the delivery of the Jewish people out of servitude in Egypt.*

5 Rosh Hashanah *is a celebration of New Year and of the act of creation of the world.*

6 Yom ha-sho'ah *is a remembrance day for the millions of people who died in the Holocaust.*

7 *The* Shema *is arguably the most significant of Jewish prayers and devout Jews repeat it twice each day.*

8 Tefillin *are leather boxes containing religious texts which Jewish men may wear on their upper arm and forehead during prayers.*

9 *Jewish men may also wear a prayer shawl during prayers and also normally wear a skull cap or yarmulkah.*

10 *In the context of Judaism, the diaspora refers to the dispersal and migration of Jews around the world, often, but not exclusively, because of persecution.*

6

Christianity

In this chapter you will learn about:
- *the development and teachings of Christianity*
- *features of Christian worship*
- *the organization of the different Christian Churches.*

History

Christianity is based upon the spiritual experience and teachings of
Jesus of Nazareth, who lived, worked and taught in Palestine some
2,000 years ago. It was a time in history and a location in which
there were a number of religious teachers who travelled and taught,
either on their own or in groups. Christianity developed within
a tradition and milieu that was Jewish and where the received
orthodoxy was Judaism. In some quarters Jesus was perceived to
be the Messiah, who was thought to have been born according to
predictions in Jewish tradition, to generate a new period in Jewish
nationhood when the will of God would prevail. The period during
which Jesus preached and developed his approach to religion and
spirituality was relatively short, about three years.

When Jesus was approximately 30 years of age he was baptized by
John the Baptist and subsequently began his ministry. Jesus asked
a total of 12 people to follow him and to become his disciples.
The disciples were of great importance in helping to disseminate

the spiritual teaching and message of Jesus. The evidence suggests that Jesus was a very skilled healer and in times of limited medical knowledge, this must have inspired enormous devotion and confidence in ordinary people. Christians believe that Jesus was the Son of God and that he was the manifestation of God on earth.

At the time of the ministry of Jesus, Palestine was a Roman colony whose ruler was Pontius Pilate. After about three years of teaching, Jesus began to alienate the Jewish authorities and his execution by crucifixion was finally authorized by Pilate. Christians believe that three days after his crucifixion Jesus was resurrected from the dead. Belief in the resurrection, based on the accounts in the four gospels, is one of the central tenets of the Christian faith.

Christianity commenced as a minority belief system within Judaism and Judaic culture. For perhaps 40 or 50 years after the death of Jesus, it appears that members of the Christian community remained largely Jewish in outlook and in their social customs, while at the same time adhering to the teachings of Jesus. This was the factor which separated them spiritually from the mainstream Jewish tradition. There was, however, a gradual tendency to begin to admit non-Jews to the Christian community. As this tendency accelerated, the Christian community moved further and further from its Jewish roots.

One of the most significant people in the early spread of the Christian message was Paul, whose original name had been Saul. Paul was born in Tarsus and came from a Jewish cultural background. He took his Jewish culture very seriously and was training to become a rabbi. To some extent this explains why he was originally so opposed to the heterodox doctrines of the early Christians and why he was involved in the persecution of Christian communities. After he experienced a vision while travelling towards Damascus, Paul became an extremely influential missionary for the developing Christian Church.

While Christianity remained as a sect or subgroup within Judaism, there existed the contentious issue of whether converts to Christianity should also have to comply with the cultural and religious requirements of Judaism. Paul was regarded by the Jewish community as extremely unorthodox in this regard because, besides encouraging orthodox Jews to become Christians, he also encouraged non-Jews or Gentiles to join the Christian community. It was this action that was regarded as subversive and which ultimately led Paul to be taken to Rome for imprisonment and trial. Paul had travelled extensively in the Mediterranean world, seeking to gain converts for Christianity, and with some success. However, it was not until the advent of Constantine as Roman Emperor that Christianity became the accepted religion of the Roman world.

Constantine, the son of Constantius, became Emperor in 312 CE. Under his rule, Christianity flourished and, indeed, Christians often received beneficial treatment within the Roman Empire. Almost inevitably, questions of interpretation and doctrine arose within the Christian faith and Constantine convened the Council of Nicea in 325 CE in order to try to clarify the nature of the concept 'Son of God' and the exact nature of the relationship between Jesus as Son of God and God the Father. The result of this Council, which was held at Nicea in present-day Turkey and attended by a large number of bishops, was the Nicene Creed, which is today used in the service of Eucharist.

Constantine also established a city to be named after him. This was Constantinople, which was established on the site of the ancient city of Byzantium on the Bosporus between Europe and Asia. Constantinople, the present-day Istanbul, was founded in 330 CE as the capital of the eastern Roman Empire.

The siting of the eastern capital so far from Rome was almost certainly one of the factors which led to the division, half way through the eleventh century, between the Eastern Orthodox Church and the Roman Catholic Church. However, some significant doctrinal differences had also developed. The Orthodox Church, for example, opposed the complete authority of the Pope. In addition, the two Churches differed in their interpretations of the nature of the Holy Spirit. The Roman Church added a phrase to the Nicene Creed which described the Holy Spirit as proceeding from the Father and the Son, instead of simply the Father. The Orthodox Church did not agree with this addition.

The Eastern Orthodox Church developed its own particular Christian culture. The Council of Chalcedon, which was held in 451 CE, established four important centres for the Orthodox Church at Constantinople, Jerusalem, Alexandria and Antioch. Constantinople was regarded as the most important of these. Each centre was administered by a patriarch, who was responsible for the work of other bishops in that region. The Orthodox Church adheres to the doctrine of Apostolic Succession in the sense that there is assumed to be a clear line of guidance and teaching from Jesus to the apostles and hence to the bishops of the Church. One of the characteristics of the Orthodox Church is the attachment to and respect for icons, or stylized religious paintings depicting Jesus and the saints.

One of the characteristic features of Christianity in Europe during the early medieval period was the growth and establishment of monasticism. From the earliest times the life of solitude and contemplation had been attractive to some Christians. St Benedict of Nursia is generally credited with being the founder of the principles of monasticism, although there had been people living a fairly solitary life of contemplation much earlier. In about 525 CE St Benedict founded the monastery of Monte Cassino and established the monastic rule of conduct for which he is well known. The 'Rule' established the principles and mode of conduct of such activities as holding collective prayers at certain times of the day, for a life consisting largely of study, work and spiritual reflection and contemplation. During this period, monasteries were the principal focus for learning and academic activity and succeeded in sustaining a tradition of Christian learning. Monasteries were the main centres of academic study. St Benedict died in about 550 CE.

After the ideological division in 1054 CE between the Orthodox Church and the Roman Catholic Church, the latter was the chief religious influence in Europe. Nonetheless, in the Mediterranean region there was increasing conflict between Christianity and Islam. One of the major results of this was the Crusades, which, while having a stated purpose, from the Christians' point of view, of regaining Palestine from the control of the Muslims, had, in addition, a perhaps less clearly stated objective of acquiring land and wealth. The support of the Pope was given for the First Crusade in 1095 CE and this succeeded in one of its aims, the capture of Jerusalem. The Second Crusade was initiated in the middle of the twelfth century and the Third Crusade, partially under the leadership of Richard I of England, set off in 1189 CE. The small gains made by the Crusades were only temporary, but there were longer-term advantages for all parties to the conflict in terms of enhanced trade and exposure to different cultural traditions. Western Europe appears to have gained considerably from contact with Islamic culture and learning.

Insight

On the downside, the Crusades have left a long legacy of a sense of cultural conflict between the Islamic and Christian worlds, which persists to some extent to this day.

From 1054 CE onwards, the Roman Catholic Church was the principal religious influence in Europe and yet gradually a sense of disquiet evolved in some quarters over practices and customs which developed in the Church. In general terms, the Church was becoming more and more influential in the secular sphere. There were also a number of events whose consequences affected the power and influence of the Church. The invention and increased use of printing and also the translation of the Bible into accessible languages had the effect of disseminating ideas and causing ordinary people to reflect on some of the customs and practices of the Church. In addition, as people began to associate themselves more and more with the country or state in which they lived, there was a concomitant tendency to reduce the level of association with the Pope and Rome. These were all gradual developments, but nevertheless worked together to create an atmosphere in which ordinary citizens were perhaps less likely to be as accepting of the power and authority of the established Church. Hence, the series of events known collectively as the Reformation started to come about.

The Reformation started in the early sixteenth century and tended to have as its early aspiration the amendment of certain practices in the Roman Catholic Church. However, it finally resulted in the establishment of the Protestant Christian tradition.

Martin Luther (1483–1546), a German theologian, was one of the significant figures of the Reformation. For historical convenience, the Reformation can be considered to have started in 1517, when he is famously said to have fixed his 95 theses to the door of the church in Wittenburg. Luther had gradually come to believe that the institution of the papacy was behaving inappropriately in a number of ways. In particular, he was very much against the selling of what were called indulgences. If someone had committed a sin and been considered to have been forgiven by God, it was often felt necessary that he or she should still receive some sort of punishment. The obtaining of an indulgence removed the necessity for such punishment. Luther felt that the sale of such indulgences was completely inappropriate. In 1520 he published *On the Babylonian Captivity of the Church of God*, in which he criticized some of the practices of the Pope. Luther was excommunicated in 1521, and placed under considerable pressure by Charles V, but did not withdraw his beliefs. Martin Luther, however, had a lasting impact. The so-called Augsburg Confession of Lutheran beliefs presented to charles V in 1530, resulted in the development of a Protestant Church. Finally, in 1555, at the so-called Peace of Augsburg, there was an agreement that the Roman Catholic Church and the Lutheran Church could exist together.

The development of Protestantism was also taking place in other parts of Europe. In Switzerland, reformers such as Zwingli in Zurich and Calvin in Geneva were having an impact. In England, under Henry VIII, the authority of the Pope was being gradually challenged and undermined. In 1534, by legislation known as the Act of Supremacy, the ruler became the head of the Church in England. Then, during the reign of Elizabeth I, the Protestant Church was declared to be the official Church of England.

During the period of the Protestant Reformation, however, the Roman Catholic Church was not unchanging. From about the middle of the sixteenth century onwards the Catholic Church went through a process of self-examination which was to some extent a response to the Reformation. This process became known as the Counter-Reformation and was an attempt to identify and correct malpractices that had arisen in the Church. One of the key events of the Counter-Reformation was when Pope Paul III convened the Council of Trent between the years 1545 and 1563. The Council was critical of the writings of Martin Luther, but also criticized some of the practices of the Church. The result was a serious attempt to reform the Church from within and to strengthen the religious belief of its members.

This was a period of considerable religious change in Europe. In England the Church of England became the established Church. Christianity had arrived in England some time before St Augustine was sent on his mission by Pope Gregory I. After the Reformation, several different strands or traditions evolved within the Church of England. Perhaps the two main ones were the 'Low' Church or Protestant tradition and the 'High' Church or wing of the Church which felt the closest affiliation with Roman Catholicism.

Currently, the Church of England is administered by the General Synod, which was established in 1970. The Church Commissioners manage the Church finances and property.

Belief system

Christianity is a monotheistic faith, believing in one God. Nevertheless, Christianity also has the concept of the Trinity, which is essentially that God has existed in and does exist in three forms. However, this does not in any way affect the essential monotheism of the religion. The Trinity consists of God as the Father, God as the Son and God as the Holy Ghost or Holy Spirit.

Insight

The Christian concept of the Trinity is perceived by some religious traditions as a dilution of the monotheistic ideal, although Christians do not see the concept as problematic.

The concept of God as Father is that God is a paternal figure who adopts a fatherly, protective attitude to all human beings. God is the creator of the world and of all things in it, but also cares for and sustains all life and living things. God, then, is seen as transcendent, as the powerful creator of the universe, but also as immanent, as the fatherly protector of human beings. God, however, has also been immanent in a different way. He sent his only son, Jesus Christ, to be born on earth as an ordinary human being and to live as a person who was eventually condemned to crucifixion for the salvation of humanity. After His execution, Jesus is believed by Christians to have been resurrected three days later and after this to have been taken up into heaven to be with God the Father. God as the Holy Spirit or Holy Ghost is, at all times, within human beings who believe in Him. The Holy Spirit sustains and supports Christian believers, helping them to lead a Christian life. It is important to recognize that the Father, Son and Holy Spirit are not three separate deities, but in Christian terms simply elements of the single, unitary God.

It is perhaps understandable that as a religion starts to develop an organization and membership, it should also wish to establish a clear and precise statement of its principal beliefs. From relatively early times, the Christian Church has attempted to do this and the statements of its belief system are generally known as 'creeds'. In the history of Christianity there have probably been a number of different creeds used at different times and by different groups, but today the two main creeds in use are the Apostles' Creed and the Nicene Creed. The Apostles' Creed was of early origin in the history of the Church, but only achieved its current form of expression in medieval times. The basic wording of the Nicene Creed was established at the Council of Nicaea in 325 CE. Although not having exactly the same content, the two creeds cover broadly the same issues of Christian doctrine and belief. They are a means of expressing in a clear and brief manner the essential matters in which Christians share a belief. They also, in a sense, define those beliefs which are to be regarded as not conforming and hence to be excluded from orthodox Christian tradition.

Christianity is a monotheistic religion, with a clear belief in one God. Jesus referred to God as 'Father' and this concept of God has been continued by Christians. This way of viewing God emphasizes the idea that God cares for humanity and protects people in the same way as a father acts towards his offspring. God is also viewed as being the most powerful entity in the universe. There is none greater than God and God has created everything in the universe, including animate and inanimate things.

Jesus is regarded by Christians as possessing all the essential qualities of God and as having come to earth from heaven in order to save human beings spiritually. Jesus is conceptualized as the Son of God. The entire purpose of Jesus' mission on earth is the spiritual redemption of humanity. Christians believe that Jesus was born to the Virgin Mary through the intervention of the Holy Spirit and when his ministry was completed he was crucified. The crucifixion has a central place in Christian belief and indeed the symbol of the cross is very widespread within the faith. It is argued that Jesus underwent the pain and suffering of the crucifixion as part of the process of forgiving the sins of all human beings. Christians believe that Jesus was resurrected from the dead three days after his execution on the cross and this provides them with an opportunity to look forward to a personal life after death, when they may be reunited with God in heaven.

It is believed that the spiritual life as defined by Jesus will continue for ever and that eventually Jesus will return to save those who have truly believed in him. If human beings will take a personal decision to believe in Jesus, they may be confident that their sins will be forgiven. Christians believe in a universal Church composed of those people who believe in God and that this Church has derived its traditions and teachings from the apostles themselves and through them from Jesus.

Some aspects of orthodox Christian belief are not universally accepted in a literal sense. An example, perhaps, is the doctrine of the virgin birth. If Jesus is perceived as the Son of God, and as coming to earth as a being of the same essence as God, it seems perhaps a reasonable assumption that his birth (the birth of a personage who is, in effect, God) would not follow the normal pattern of human conception. However, such a conception and birth are not explicable by natural science and hence a Christian has difficulty explaining this doctrine to a non-believer. For this reason some Christians do not concentrate very much on the mechanism of the birth of Jesus, but rather focus on the significance of the event for the world and for humanity and the reason for Jesus being born.

Some of the most important aspects of Christian belief derive from the events surrounding the death and resurrection of Jesus Christ. The Last Supper has given rise to perhaps the most significant Christian sacrament, that of the Eucharist, Mass or Holy Communion. When Jesus entered Jerusalem near the end of his life, it was the period of the celebration of Passover. Jesus sat with his disciples and took bread and wine. Although this was the norm and there was nothing unusual in this, Jesus converted the eating of bread and drinking of wine into a ceremony of great significance. As he broke the bread he asked the disciples to regard it as his body. Similarly, the wine was to be regarded as his blood. It is a reasonable assumption that Jesus had a premonition of his imminent death and wanted to provide a metaphor by which his disciples could remember him. The bread was to represent his body, which would be beaten and then nailed to the cross, and the wine would represent his blood, which would be shed during his punishment and execution. The replication of this image during the Eucharist has remained powerful image for Christians to this day.

It seems a reasonable assumption that Jesus could have avoided the
sequence of events which led up to his conviction and crucifixion
and yet he chose not to do so. The crucifixion is viewed by many
Christians as a demonstration of the way in which Jesus loved
all human beings. It was an opportunity for him to suffer and to
sacrifice himself in order to forgive the collective sins of humanity.
For many Christians the crucifixion was a form of self-sacrifice
through which means Jesus was able to take upon himself the
suffering which was due to collective humanity for their sins. This
is the type of symbolism which many Christians attach to the event
of the crucifixion and which makes it such a potent event for those
who believe in Jesus and his teachings.

Joseph of Arimathaea obtained the permission of Pontius Pilate
to take the body of Jesus. The body was placed in a tomb owned
by Joseph and the entrance to the tomb was sealed. Three days
later, the body of Jesus had disappeared from the tomb. Christians
believe that Jesus was resurrected by God, that he then made
several appearances and subsequently ascended into heaven to be
with God.

This is the core of what Christians believe. The events of the
resurrection may, of course, be subjected to a range of speculation
and critical analysis. There are no witnesses to the events in the
tomb. If one wanted to consider possible scientific explanation of
a 'resurrection' one might consider, for example, that Jesus did

not actually die on the cross, but went into a form of coma. He then perhaps became conscious during the next three days and, either by himself or with the aid of friends, moved the stone sealing the entrance and escaped. There are many other feasible, rational explanations. Nevertheless, such explanations are less significant for committed Christians, for whom the resurrection is a reality and a reality that demonstrates the power of God.

Some Christian organizations do not necessarily adhere to this broadly agreed doctrinal position. One example is the Quaker faith, or as it is more correctly known, the Religious Society of Friends. Founded in the seventeenth century by a group of people among whom George Fox is often regarded as the principal figure, the Quakers have resisted the idea of having an agreed set of religious tenets. The faith developed among people who, although originally Christian, had become dissatisfied with many features of Christian practice and belief. To this day, many 'Friends' as they are often called, still regard themselves as Christian, although many others would prefer to regard themselves as believing in a more general divine presence rather than a specifically Christian God. Friends generally believe that 'the Divine' is present in all of us, and that an understanding of that presence can best be gained during periods of quiet contemplation. The latter is the normal form of religious practice held in the Friends' Meeting Houses. The broad assumption of a spiritual presence in all human beings has been perhaps one factor in the well-known role of Quakers in the peace movement, in working towards helping the disadvantaged, and in exhibiting an approach of tolerance to humanity in general.

Organization

There are a number of significant differences between the different Christian Churches, both in terms of administrative organization and in terms of religious worship and practice. The Church of England is known as the 'established' Church in England. This term signifies that it is the Church which is integrated with different aspects of the governance of the country, including for example officiating at the coronation of a new king or queen. The Church of England can trace its origins back to the period of the Celts and even earlier to the Romans. Nevertheless, its foundation is also often associated with the missionary work of St Augustine. The term Anglican Communion refers to the 38 Churches, in different parts of the world, that share matters of religious doctrine and worship with the Church of England. These Churches often have a historical link with England connected with the history of British colonialism and the Commonwealth. The Lambeth Conference is the gathering every ten years of the bishops from the constituent Churches of the Anglican Communion. The Conference was instituted in 1867 CE.

The Church of England is divided into two areas, one administered by the Archbishop of York and the other by the Archbishop of Canterbury. These areas are in turn subdivided into over 40 dioceses. The principal decision-making body of the Church of England is the General Synod, which was established in 1970. The Synod is divided into three so-called 'houses', namely the House of Laity, the House of Clergy and the House of Bishops. In 1992 the General Synod agreed to the ordination of women priests, and the first women were ordained in 1994. The Synod has the power to propose laws on issues which relate to the Church of England, but these must be approved by parliament.

Insight

The position of women in the Church of England remains to some degree a matter of contention, particularly in relation to the notion of women bishops, but the Church does seem to be moving towards the fuller integration of women within the Church hierarchy.

The Roman Catholic Church is led by the Bishop of Rome, otherwise known as the Pope, who is regarded as having inherited the authority originally given by Jesus Christ to St Peter. The latter was the first Bishop of Rome. The title 'Pope' is of more recent origin, having been employed first in 1073 CE. The Pope exercises spiritual authority over the Catholic Church, but in addition administers the Vatican City State, which was established in 1929. The Vatican State includes such well-known places as St Peter's Square and the Vatican Palace. Since the time of the first Vatican Council held in 1870, the Pope has been assumed always to be correct when he makes statements on religious matters as the Pope. This teaching of the Church is known as papal infallibility. Historically, the papacy has exercised considerable secular authority. From the period of Pope Leo III and Charlemagne, the Pope was a significant authority in Europe, although his secular powers diminished somewhat during and after the Reformation.

Within the Vatican, the leading governing body of the Catholic Church is the Sacred College of Cardinals. The *curia*, or papal court, is a complex administrative structure of committees and bodies designed to administer the Church, with key functions and positions normally occupied by cardinals. The powers of the curia are given to it by the Pope. A *papal nuncio* is the term given to a member of the diplomatic service which is organized from the Vatican. In England the Bishop's Conference is the prime decision-making body for the Roman Catholic Church and is led by the Archbishop of Westminster.

Both the Roman Catholic Church and the Church of England have a process of endorsing formal membership during a ceremony known as confirmation. This process takes place when the individual is older than at baptism and hence able to make mature decisions. Confirmation involves a bishop laying hands on the individual who is becoming a full member of the Church. Many Christians hold the view that it is during this ceremony that the Holy Spirit enters the individual. Baptist churches retain the view that baptism as a process should be reserved for adults who are in a position to understand fully the implications of what they are doing and saying. Adult baptism of this type usually involves full immersion in water, often in a purpose-built pool.

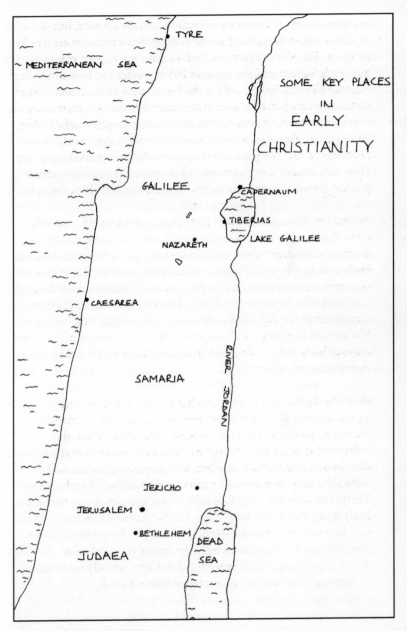

Figure 6.1 Some key places in early Christianity.

Some aspects of Christian worship are especially significant and act as metaphors for key features of religious doctrine. These are known as *sacraments* and examples are baptism and the Eucharist. During Mass, for example, the wafer and the wine represent the body and blood of Jesus respectively, in relation to his death on the cross. They act as a reminder of the death of Jesus and the reasons for Jesus sacrificing his life for humanity. Different Churches regard a different number of aspects of worship as sacramental in nature. This relates to some extent to matters of belief and practice in a particular Church. The Eucharist is arguably the most important aspect of collective Christian practice and it is generally believed by most Christians that during the celebration of the Eucharist, Jesus is present in some spiritual form. The belief and doctrine concerning the precise form in which Jesus is present during the Eucharist are not the same in different religious traditions. Roman Catholicism has the doctrine, for example, that the bread and wine during the Eucharist are actually *transubstantiated* or changed in 'substance' into the body and blood of Jesus. Other Christians may adopt a more general view that Jesus is present in some rather more unspecified spiritual form.

A particular feature of Christian organization is the detailed manner in which the calendar year is subdivided and named to correspond with key Christian festivals. The Church year has evolved over the centuries, with different seasons and days being associated with particular types of Christian celebration. It was fairly early in the history of Christianity, for example, probably by about the second century CE, that Sunday became the principal day of Christian worship. Lent probably has its origins in the establishment of a period of time prior to Easter, in which relatively new converts to Christianity were given tuition in the faith and prepared themselves for their baptism at Easter.

The first period of the Christian year can be thought of as Advent, a name which derives from the Latin *adventus*, meaning the 'coming'. This period encourages Christians to prepare for Christmas and the remembrance of the birth of Jesus. The origin of the celebration of Christmas on 25 December can be dated back to 336 CE. There were probably mid-winter celebrations and festivities around this period in various societies prior to the development of Christianity. The next festival after Christmas is Twelfth Day or Epiphany. This festival is a celebration of the three wise men travelling to see Jesus. The night before Epiphany is known as Twelfth Night and there is a long tradition of holding festivities on that night and of giving presents.

Lent developed historically into a period when people fasted as a spiritual preparation for remembering the crucifixion of Jesus at Easter. Originally, there was a real sense of fasting during Lent and people would give up certain pleasures or eat only very simple food. Gradually, however, Lent has become less and less celebrated in a formal sense. The period of Lent commences with Ash Wednesday which is so called because originally people placed ashes on their forehead to remind them of the coming sacrifices of Lent. Lent lasts for 40 days.

Easter is the next main Christian festival and marks the remembrance of the crucifixion and resurrection of Jesus. There has historically been some debate about determining the date of Easter. At the Council of Nicaea in 325 CE it was decided that Easter would be dated by association with the spring equinox and could be between 22 March and 25 April. The Ascension is a remembrance of Jesus returning to heaven and being reunited with the Father.

Whit Sunday is normally the seventh Sunday after Easter and is a celebration of the event of the Holy Spirit coming down out of heaven and inspiring the apostles. Whit Sunday is also known as Pentecost and had its origins in a Jewish ceremony to celebrate a successful wheat harvest. The term Whit Sunday originates in 'White' Sunday, signifying this date as being typically associated with baptismal ceremonies and the accompanying white garments. Corpus Christi is a perhaps slightly less well-known festival, normally held on the second Thursday after Whit Sunday and celebrating the Holy Eucharist. In the thirteenth century CE, it was changed from being a fairly localized festival to one celebrated throughout the Christian Church.

The Christian Churches have their own laws which govern matters concerning, for example, the conduct of the clergy and matters of Christian belief. This body of legislation is known as canon law. It can be traced back to the decisions taken by the bishops in the early years of the Church. These laws and rulings eventually became included in the *Codex Juris Canonici*, or the compilation of rulings of the Roman Catholic Church. The Anglican Church had its principal laws collected in the so-called *Book of Canons*, in the seventeenth century CE.

The Christian Church which developed in the first few centuries after the death of Jesus perhaps understandably did not remain as a uniform organization, but evolved as a result of both internal and external factors. Indeed, it is rather unclear exactly what form of organization Jesus himself envisaged developing after his death. As different perceptions of doctrine and belief emerged, an increasing number of 'Churches' developed as time passed. Eventually, however, it became clear that there were a number of disadvantages in having so many different denominations and Churches. The development of Church missions in the nineteenth century highlighted the difficulties and apparent inconsistencies in having missionaries from a large number of different doctrinal backgrounds. Pressures such as these led to the creation of such organizations as the Edinburgh Missionary Conference in 1910 and the general ecumenical movement which strove for greater unity of the different Churches. This trend was instrumental in the establishment of the World Council of Churches at Amsterdam in 1948. This organization, whose headquarters are in Geneva in Switzerland, has over 200 different Churches as members. The involvement of the Roman Catholic Church in the ecumenical movement was given considerable impetus by the establishment of the Second Vatican Council by Pope John XXIII. There continues to be significant progress in the search for commonalities among the different Christian Churches of the world.

10 THINGS TO REMEMBER

1 *Christianity is a monotheistic religion.*

2 *According to Christians, Jesus Christ is the Son of God.*

3 *He was crucified, but Christians believe that, having died, he was resurrected from the dead.*

4 *Most Christians believe that God exists as three distinct 'persons': Father, Son and Holy Ghost.*

5 *Christians believe that those who have faith in the message of Jesus Christ will, after death, attain everlasting life.*

6 *The Roman Catholic Church accepts the authority of the Pope.*

7 *Protestant Churches evolved from the dispute with Roman Catholicism in the sixteenth century.*

8 *The Apostles' Creed and the Nicene Creed are succinct statements of Christian belief and doctrine.*

9 *The Church of England is the 'established' church in England.*

10 *In 1992 the General Synod of the Church of England accepted that women could be ordained as priests.*

7

Islam

In this chapter you will learn about:
- *the life of Muhammad*
- *the principal teachings and practices of Islam*
- *the importance of the Qur'an in Islam*.

History

Islam began as a religion and developed in Arabia in the early seventh century CE. Its development was particularly associated with two cities, Mecca and Yathrib. The latter city was later known as Medina. The Arabia of the time was a tribal society, many people leading a relatively nomadic life, with some groups settling around oases and wells, leading to the development of towns and cities. The tribe was the principal social group and each tribe was divided into smaller groupings of families and relatives, called clans. The tribe was very important in terms of ensuring social solidarity. Individuals owed a strong sense of allegiance to their tribe and in return, the tribe as a collective unity offered protection to the individual. One of the important aspects of ethics at the time was to reinforce the sense of individual loyalty to the tribe.

One of the main occupations of the sixth and seventh centuries in Arabia was trade, with camel caravans being the principal means of transport. Mecca became important as a commercial centre largely through being located on caravan routes. There was also a certain amount of agriculture around the oases and the keeping of grazing animals was also important. Arabia at this time provided a harsh physical environment and the virtues that were particularly esteemed within tribal culture included courage, bravery and loyalty to friends and relatives.

The predominant tribe in the area of Mecca was the *Quraysh* tribe. Besides being a commercial centre, Mecca was also important as a religious centre and the Quraysh had gained from this. In Mecca was located a religious shrine called the *Kaaba*, which housed among others things symbols of the divinities of Arabia. People traditionally made pilgrimages to Mecca to see the Kaaba and this large number of regular visitors to the city inevitably increased the economic prosperity of the Quraysh. Arabia could legitimately be described as a polytheistic society, although tribal mores and morality were arguably a more potent force than religion.

Muhammad received a series of spiritual revelations from God and these formed the religious basis of Islam. In the early days of the development of Islam, some people were opposed to the new faith, but Muhammad managed to place the faith upon firm foundations in his lifetime. Muhammad was born in Mecca in 570 CE as a member of the Hashim clan and his early life was not easy. Muhammad's father died before his son was born and Muhammad's mother died when he was six years old. This must have been difficult for the young boy, even though he did have the support of an extended family. Muhammad was cared for initially by his grandfather and then by an uncle, Abu Talib. It seems probable that Abu Talib sought to teach Muhammad the skills of adulthood by taking him on trading journeys by caravan, and on one occasion it is likely that Muhammad went on a journey to Syria.

Probably because of his developing skills in trade, a widow named Khadija asked Muhammad to manage one of her caravans for her. She was a woman of considerable wealth and also

experienced in matters of commerce and trade. Muhammad proved
to be extremely capable and although there was an age difference
between them (Khadija being about 40 years old and Muhammad
about 25) they married. According to tradition, Khadija bore seven
children to Muhammad, although three of them died when very
young. Muhammad gradually grew more and more respected in
Meccan society, not merely because of his success in business, but
also because he was recognized as being scrupulously honest in his
dealings with people.

There seems little doubt that Muhammad was of a religious
disposition and enjoyed meditation and reflective thought.
He regularly went away on his own to a cave outside Mecca where
he was able to contemplate spiritual matters quietly. At about the
age of 40 years Muhammad had a spiritual vision while meditating
in the cave and an angel spoke to him. Muhammad felt that this
was the angel Gabriel and that the angel was communicating
to him the word of God. This was the first of many revelations
experienced by Muhammad. When they first occurred, he discussed
them with his wife Khadija and with one or two close friends.
They accepted the seriousness and validity of the revelations and,
perhaps partly as a result of this response, Muhammad formed
the opinion that he had been chosen by God as the recipient of
divine revelations. These revelations occurred from time to time
for the duration of Muhammad's life. He memorized them and
then they were committed to writing, either by Muhammad on his
own or with the help of others. These written revelations were to
become the *Qur'an*. It is significant that Muhammad always made
clear that he did not regard himself as the writer or originator of
the Qur'an. He always emphasized that the Qur'an was the work
of God.

In approximately 613 CE, Muhammad started to convey the
content of some of his revelations to a wider public. Until then
he had only spoken of these matters to family and close friends.
Some people found the content of Muhammad's message very
appealing, particularly in the sense that a single god was the source
of all power and goodness in the world. This message probably

had particular attractions for the poorer people in society, rather than some of the tribal leaders who already exerted considerable power and influence. There was a sense in which Muhammad's message tended to provide a challenge to those in power. This was particularly so in relation to the tribal system. Each individual tended to look to the tribal unit to provide a sense of belonging within society. Yet Muhammad's message was that Islam transcended tribal groupings. Hence, those who led the tribes were not necessarily in favour of a world view which saw the tribal unit as secondary in importance to a community of Muslim believers.

These differences of view about Muhammad's message led to a certain degree of persecution of the Muslims in Mecca. It was clear that it would be difficult for Muhammad to remain in Mecca indefinitely and it was fortunate that 12 visitors from the nearby city of Yathrib heard Muhammad preaching and agreed to offer support and protection to him and the growing Muslim community. In fact, they needed someone of social standing to act as an intermediary in resolving a dispute between two tribes in Yathrib and felt that Muhammad could fulfil that role. The year was 621 CE and Muhammad and his followers began to make plans for the move to Yathrib. These plans were made in secret, for the Muslims presumably feared further persecution.

Towards the end of 622 CE most of the Muslim community had managed to travel to Yathrib and settle there. The only Muslims left in Mecca were Muhammad, his cousin Ali and his close friend Abu Bakr who was later to become his father-in-law. The Meccan leaders were eager to capture Muhammad, but he left secretly with Abu Bakr, and Ali followed later. Eventually, all three were successful in reaching Yathrib. The escape of the Muslim community from Mecca is regarded as a very important event in Muslim history and in fact the Muslim calendar is dated from this event which took place in 622 CE. The escape from Mecca is known as the *Hijra*. The city of Yathrib was later given the name of Medina, a term which may be translated as 'City of the Prophet'.

Muhammad was now becoming more important as a political leader as well as being the spiritual leader of the Muslims. When he had settled in Medina, he married Aisha and Hafsa who were the daughters of Abu Bakr and another of his followers, Umar. The Meccans, however, had not forgotten about the Muslims and saw them as a continuing challenge to their power and trade. There was openly acknowledged conflict between the two cities and, during the years 623 CE and 624 CE, there were a number of raids and battles between the two sides, particularly attacks on trading caravans. At the battle of Badr in 624 CE, the Muslim army was victorious over the Meccans. In 625 CE the Meccans mounted an assault upon Medina, but this was repulsed. Again in 627 CE the Meccans unsuccessfully tried to besiege Medina.

In 630 CE Muhammad marched on Mecca with a large army and the Meccans surrendered. Muhammad entered Mecca without any violence against the people. He had the different religious images removed from the Kaaba and encouraged the Meccans to become Muslims. He then returned to Medina. The people of Mecca converted to Islam over a period of time. In early 632 CE Muhammad made what was to be his final pilgrimage to Mecca and delivered a sermon which became known as his 'Farewell Sermon'. This pilgrimage made by Muhammad became the model for the institution of the *Hajj*, or pilgrimage, which all Muslims are expected to make to Mecca. Muhammad died a few months later in 632 CE.

After the death of Muhammad it was not immediately clear who would be his successor. Some people disagreed about whether Muhammad had expressed a wish concerning the person who would succeed him. Eventually Abu Bakr was selected as the successor. He had a broad spectrum of support and during his lifetime, Muhammad had asked Abu Bakr to lead the Friday prayers whenever he was unable to do so. Abu Bakr was known as the first Caliph, a term which may be approximately translated as 'successor'. After the death of Muhammad, the first four caliphs were Abu Bakr (caliph from 632 CE to 634 CE), Umar (634 CE to 644 CE), Uthman (644 CE to 656 CE) and Ali (656 CE to 661 CE). Under these four caliphs there was a period of very rapid expansion of Islam. First of all the main tribes within Arabia were converted to the principles of Islam, and then the Muslim faith was taken in a relatively short period of time to neighbouring countries in the Middle East. The fourth Caliph, Ali, was the son-in-law of Muhammad. He was married to Fatima, the daughter of Muhammad and his first wife Khadija. Ali and Fatima had two sons, Husayn and Hasan. The supporters of Ali felt that he should have been the first caliph and that he had been wrongfully overlooked in the first place.

The caliph Uthman had been assassinated in 656 CE and Ali came under some criticism because he had not managed to prosecute those responsible for the murder. This may have been one cause for the revolts that took place against his leadership. One revolt was led by the daughter of Abu Bakr, named Aisha; another was led by Muawiyah, who was a relative of the caliph Uthman and also Governor of Syria. Ali was himself assassinated in 661 CE and Muawiyah became the caliph. The leadership of the Muslim community passed to the so-called Umayyad dynasty which was based in Damascus in Syria. This dynasty was eventually succeeded by the Abbasid dynasty based in Baghdad. During the Abbasid period there was a great flowering of Islamic culture. However, in 1258 CE Baghdad was attacked and defeated by Mongol invaders. Although these people were originally non-Muslims, they eventually became converted to the faith. By the seventeenth century Islam had reached its zenith in terms of expansion. As Western Europe made greater technological advances and achieved greater military power, there was increased competition with the Islamic world. Europe was attempting to extend its colonies, leading to confrontation of the type experienced in India between the existing Mughal empire and the British.

Belief system

The prophet Muhammad received a series of religious revelations. Muslims believe that these revelations came from God. At the time of the revelations, they were either memorized and/or written down and then later compiled into the sacred book known as the Qur'an. Muslims believe that God has in heaven an original book from which the revelations received by Muhammad are taken. The sayings of the Qur'an are regarded as God's actual words and hence, as they are in Arabic, there is a special significance attached to that language. So great is this significance that many Muslims feel that it is wrong to translate the Qur'an into any other language. Not only is the language itself very important, but also the content of the Qur'an is felt to be the complete revelation of God to human beings. God will not reveal anything else beyond the Qur'an. Muhammad is regarded by Muslims as the medium through which God's revelations reach humanity. The Qur'an is not regarded in any sense as the work of Muhammad, but as the direct word of God.

The Qur'an contains 114 chapters, or *suras*. These are predominantly arranged in terms of length, with the longer chapters normally coming nearer the beginning of the Qur'an. Some Muslims believe that the chapters are in an order that reflects God's wishes. The chapters are divided into verses called *ayat*. The word 'Qur'an' means approximately 'to recite', and the ability to recite the Qur'an well is regarded as a great skill. Some devout Muslims attempt to memorize the entire Qur'an and success at this is regarded as a great achievement. Such a person is known as *hafiz*.

As Muhammad experienced his revelations, they were generally written down and also memorized. Later the different revelations were collected together into the Qur'an. There is some dispute about exactly when this took place. Some argue that it took place under the authority of Abu Bakr, while others suggest it was at the time of Umar. The modern consensus is that the

Qur'an in its present form was prepared under the caliph Uthman. Muslims believe that the content of the Qur'an cannot be changed in any way because it comes directly from God and that it is the final divine revelation.

Adherents of Islam have five principal duties which they are obliged to fulfil as part of the faith. These are usually termed the Five Pillars. The first of these is known as the Profession of Faith, or *Shahada*. All Muslims are expected to make the following statement, which is a summary of what it means to be a Muslim. The statement is: 'There is no god but the God and Muhammad is the messenger of the God.' This sentence is to be uttered by people when they become Muslims by conversion and is also the principal means by which an individual asserts his or her adherence to Islam. In particular, the Shahada emphasizes the fact that for Muslims there is only one God and that this monotheism is central to the faith.

The second of the Five Pillars is ritual prayer. Muslims may pray to God at any time in the day, but this specific requirement means that five times a day a Muslim should pray using a certain form of words while facing in the direction of Mecca. The prayers are also accompanied by certain forms of kneeling and prostrations. This form of prayer is known as *salat*. Before the prayer starts, the individual should engage in ritual washing. This is designed to create a sense of spiritual cleanliness prior to prayer, rather than actually washing for the purpose of physical cleanliness. The term for this ritual washing is *wudu*. If the Muslim is performing the salat in a location outside or away from a mosque, then as clean and peaceful a place as possible will be selected and a prayer mat will be placed on the ground as a symbol of spiritual cleanliness.

Ritual prayers take place on five occasions during the day: at daybreak, midday, the middle of the afternoon, at sunset and during the evening. One of the most famous sounds of Islamic culture is related to the salat, in that traditionally it is the *muezzin* who calls the Muslims from the minaret of the mosque to attend the prayers. The main prayer time of the week is at noon on Fridays and for these prayers it is normal for people to attend the mosque, when the prayers will be said by the *imam*. There will usually also be a sermon which typically discusses a few verses from the Qur'an.

The next of the Five Pillars is the giving of alms. This is termed *zakat*. Again Muslims may give money or goods to charity at any time, but zakat is regarded as a requirement. It normally consists of giving two and a half per cent of one's income, and perhaps other assets, to charity or deserving causes. The percentage can sometimes be more in some communities and may be as high as ten per cent. There may also be some flexibility and variation in the income and goods which form the basis of the zakat. Communities may differ somewhat in this respect also.

There are variations in how the zakat is donated. Sometimes it is the custom to give the money to the mosque in the area, which then arranges distribution to needy causes. In other communities, people act individually to distribute the money in the way they feel appropriate. Finally, there are some societies in which the zakat is a form of tax, collected centrally by the government. The concept of zakat involves the view that the wealth gained by individuals results ultimately from the generosity of God and hence people have a responsibility to redistribute that wealth to those who are needy. The zakat collected will be used not only to support those in financial need, but also to help with passing the message of Islam on to others.

The fourth Pillar is the duty to fast during the month of *Ramadan*, which is the ninth month of the Islamic calendar. The fast is observed from sunrise to sunset for a total of 30 days. During that period every day all adult Muslims should not take any food or drink. The transition from night to day and vice versa, at the beginning and end of the day, is often defined by being able/unable to distinguish between a black and a white cotton thread held together. The fast is not easy to maintain, particularly when one considers that in many Muslim countries it is very hot and abstaining from food and drink during the day makes great demands upon the individual. Ramadan is a period when Muslims demonstrate great discipline, both in a physical sense and in a spiritual sense, and also contemplate God and the religious life.

Insight

Even in Western countries where the extremes of temperature may not be as great as in Arabia, maintaining the fast is still very demanding, and is a formidable test, both physically and spiritually.

At sunset each day during Ramadan, Muslims eat a light snack which breaks the fast, and then later in the evening there is a much more substantial meal taken in the company of family members. During the evening people usually try to visit the mosque for prayers and for the special events that are held during this month. After a night's sleep, people get up in sufficient time before sunrise in order to eat the first meal of the day, which will have to suffice until the evening. Towards the end of Ramadan there are special celebrations. One of these is the celebration of the so-called 'Night of Power', which is the first night during which Muhammad received a revelation from God. The 'Night of Power' is remembered on the 27th day of the month of Ramadan. The conclusion of the fast of Ramadan is a time of great celebration, when family members gather and give each other presents. This festival is known as *Eid ul-Fitr*.

The final Pillar of Islam is the pilgrimage to Mecca, which is known as the *Hajj*. Although the event is held every year at approximately the same time, the duty of Muslims is to make the pilgrimage at least once during their lives. The Hajj is held during the 12th month of the Islamic calendar, between certain specified days. It is possible for Muslims to make a pilgrimage to Mecca at any time, without perhaps the visits to the associated religious sites. This is termed a 'Lesser Pilgrimage' and is not regarded as being equivalent to the full Hajj. In 632 CE Muhammad completed a Hajj to Mecca and it was on this occasion that most of the traditional, celebratory features of the pilgrimage were defined. All adult

Muslims are expected to complete the Hajj, provided that they are not unwell and also have the money to pay for the trip. In earlier times, before the advent of modern transport, it was arguably a bigger undertaking, with land caravans taking a long time to make the journey. People making the Hajj could be absent from families for a long time and the journey could be dangerous. They would have had to make arrangements for the care and support of their families while they were absent.

Those on the pilgrimage visit Mecca and the neighbouring towns and sites of religious significance in the history of Islam. There are certain prescriptions in terms of dress and other preparations for the visit to Mecca. Men wear long white sheets of cloth and shave their heads and women may wear a simple, long white dress, and also keep their heads covered. At Mecca pilgrims first visit the Kaaba, which is a large cube-shaped building covered in a black cloth at the time of the Hajj. In one corner of it, there is a black stone which was said to have been given to Ibrahim (Abraham) by the angel Jibril (Gabriel). The Kaaba is situated in the Grand Mosque in Mecca. Pilgrims walk around the Kaaba seven times, moving in an anti-clockwise direction. Having completed the circumambulation of the Kaaba, pilgrims then move on to the two small hills of Safa and Marwah. They either walk as quickly as they can or run between these two hills. This act is in remembrance of the mother of Ismail running backwards and forwards seeking water. As tradition has it, while she was doing this, the young Ismail was kicking his feet and in doing so scraped away the sand, revealing a spring of water which became known as *Zamzam*.

The Hajj consists of a series of predetermined visits and ceremonies and the next one is for pilgrims to visit the Plain of Arafat and in particular, Mount Mercy. This is where tradition holds that Muhammad preached his final sermon. From midday until sunset on the day of the visit, pilgrims stand in contemplation of God. Having visited the Plain of Arafat, pilgrims then travel back in the direction of Mecca. They stop at Muzdalifah and then Mina. At this last location there are three pillars which for Muslims are representative of evil in the world and at which pilgrims ceremonially throw stones. When they return to Mecca for the conclusion of the Hajj, there is a large festival called *Eid ul-Adha*. Although this concludes the actual Hajj, some pilgrims then make the journey to Medina, in order to visit the place where Muhammad was buried. Making the Hajj pilgrimage is regarded as so significant for Muslims that people who have made the journey are allowed to add a title to their names. This title is *Hajji* for men and *Hajjah* for women.

Although the Hajj completes the so-called Five Pillars, some Muslims feel that informally one may consider a sixth pillar to be the concept of *jihad* or struggle. Some people gain the impression that jihad signifies fighting or a battle, but this is by no means so. It is true that in the early history of Islam, particularly in the disputes between the populations of Medina and Mecca, Muslims did do battle in order to defend their faith. However, physical warfare is not the only meaning of jihad. It can also mean the psychological and spiritual struggle within the minds and hearts of people, against the evil both within themselves and within society at large. Jihad can signify any activity which represents a struggle to support Islam. Hence, although jihad is not an official pillar of Islam, nevertheless, all Muslims are expected to 'fight' to further the faith and to defend it against any acts that might seek to undermine it.

Insight
The term jihad has almost passed into popular usage, but it is important to recognize that its principal meaning is the moral struggle against evil in the world, and the struggle of the individual to lead an ethical life.

Many religions have developed mystical elements that exist alongside what might be called the orthodox strand of the faith. In the case of Islam, the mystical strand is known as *Sufism*. This is a path of knowledge and discipline by which the aspirant seeks a direct understanding and experience of God. Again, as perhaps in other faiths, there has been an uneasy coexistence between orthodox, traditional Islam and Sufism. Some traditional Muslims may well have felt that Sufism represented a challenge to received tradition. Contrariwise, some Sufis may have considered that their practices offered a means of renewing long-term tradition.

> ## Insight
> Debate between mystic and orthodox branches of religions are relatively common: for example, between Christian mystics and the established Churches, and between the traditions of Kabbalah and orthodox Judaism, as well as between Sufism and orthodox Islam.

The word *Sufi* is probably derived from the Arabic *suf*, meaning 'wool'. The relevance of this is that the early Sufis would often wear a simple woollen cloak. In fact, simplicity of lifestyle has always tended to be one of the hallmarks of Sufism. Traditionally, Sufis have led an ascetic lifestyle characterized by the possession of few belongings and by fasting regularly. They have held to the view that they should try to avoid desires for material things and felt that by abandoning worldly desires, they would arrive at a state of knowing God more closely. Certainly, many Sufis felt an affinity with what they saw as the virtues of the lifestyle at the time of Muhammad. This was seen as being an age when the true principles of Islam were able to flourish.

The *shaikh*, or spiritual teacher, has tended to have a very important role in Sufism. The shaikh is a person of accepted spirituality, who has a knowledge of Islam and the Qur'an and is able to provide religious advice and training to those who gather around him. It is part of the principle of the role of the shaikh that he passes on his spiritual understanding to his disciples who, in turn as they grow older, themselves take on disciples. Thus there is a sense of spiritual tradition that passes on from generation to generation. Many shaikhs assert that their ancestry can be traced back to religious teachers who were alive at the time of Muhammad and hence to Muhammad himself. Therefore, there is a claim that in some cases a form of religious lineage exists which can be traced forwards and backwards through the centuries from shaikh to shaikh.

It has been the normal pattern for religious communities to grow up around a well-known shaikh. The shaikh would provide spiritual tuition and guidance not only to his disciples but also to laypeople living in the vicinity. Each community might typically consist of a core of full-time disciples who would in effect be religious ascetics. They would submit themselves to the Sufi discipline and perhaps eventually become teachers themselves. The community would typically be supported by a group of laypeople who would supply donations of food and physical requisites to sustain the community.

Again as with the mystical elements in other faiths, the Sufis have tended to reject the external forms and customs of orthodox religious tradition. They have sought to gain a direct experience of God, unencumbered by the practices of the mainstream tradition. In order to achieve this they have used a number of spiritual techniques. They have used extended periods of prayer and of meditation on the texts of the Qur'an. One of the favoured techniques is that of *dhikr* or 'remembering'. This signifies a practice by which one of the names of God is repeated over and over again as a form of spiritual meditation. Some Sufis have claimed that one of the purposes of the practice and discipline is to achieve a form of union with God. When expressed in some ways, such claims have at times been viewed as heretical by orthodox Islam and those expressing such ideas have been subject to strong criticism and indeed punishment.

One of the best-known Sufi mystics was Al-Ghazali, who was born in Tus in Iran in the early eleventh century CE. He was extremely learned and wrote a large number of books. He became a professor in Baghdad and developed a reputation for his teaching and writing. In 1095 CE he reached a point in his life when he became rather dissatisfied with the relatively comfortable life he had created for himself and decided to make a break from his existing lifestyle. He assumed the life of a wandering Sufi mystic, carrying with him only the most basic of possessions. Having visited Syria, Jerusalem and Mecca, he eventually returned to Iran, where he established a Sufi community. In later life, he did in fact return to teaching, but died in 1111 CE. Probably his best-known work is *The Revival of the Religious Sciences*.

Organization

The mosque, or *masjid* to use the Arabic word, is a central feature in the Muslim community. It has historically been more than a place of prayer and many mosques have had further buildings attached to them, for a variety of additional purposes. The mosque has been the place where children received religious tuition and where people of all ages were taught more about the Qur'an and learned to read, write and speak Arabic. It has, moreover, been a place at which members of the Islamic community could meet; where people could go for a period of quiet contemplation; or where they could discuss religious ideas. Many mosques had schools associated with them and some mosques further functioned as law courts.

Most mosques have a recognizable architecture involving a large open space for prayer meetings, often a dome, and one or more minarets. It is from the latter that the muezzin calls Muslims to prayer at the mosque. The basic design of the mosque is modelled on that of Muhammad's house in Medina. One significant feature of the mosque is that it does not contain any pictures on the walls or any human images. There may be inscriptions from the Qur'an on the walls of the mosque, and the floor of the prayer room may well be carpeted, but there will not be statues of any kind.
The prayer room will not contain any chairs, tables or other furniture. Muslims pray facing towards Mecca and set into the wall of the mosque will be a niche, or *mihrab*, which is in the direction of Mecca. There is usually a wooden pulpit, or *minbar*, from which the sermon is delivered, for example, at the prayers at noon on Fridays, when the Muslim community gathers as a congregation at the mosque. The Friday attendance is regarded as important by Muslims. It is primarily men who attend, but some women may also do so. In this case, they usually pray separately from the men.

It is normal for people to engage in ritual washing prior to ritual prayer and for this reason the mosque usually provides a room with water taps in it. Shoes are also removed before entering the prayer room. It is not compulsory for Muslims to attend the mosque for *salat* or ritual prayer, although it is regarded as particularly desirable to attend the Friday noon prayers.

Insight

The design of the mosque tends to reflect the virtue of simplicity which is a feature of Islam. This is seen in the lack of ostentation in the décor, and in the absence of human images, which allows the believer to concentrate upon the nature of the one God.

Although one can identify a body of shared belief among all Muslims, there have nevertheless been differences in terms of the way the faith has evolved. This has resulted in the development of two main groups, the Sunni Muslims and the Shi'ite Muslims. The historical difference between them can be traced back to a fundamental disagreement about who should have led the Muslim community after the death of Muhammad.

The Shi'ite Muslims feel that when Muhammad died, Ali, his cousin and son-in-law, should have been the leader of the community. In fact, there were three caliphs before Ali had the opportunity to be caliph, but Shi'ite Muslims do not regard them as having been rightful and legitimate leaders. When Uthman, the third caliph, died and Ali was made caliph, not all Muslims were united behind him. Indeed, there were some Muslims who supported Muawiya, a cousin of Uthman, to be leader of the community. Ultimately, there was violent confrontation between the two groups, which resulted in the murder of Ali in 661 CE. Muawiya was able to take control of the community. He became caliph and founded an Islamic dynasty known as the Umayyads. However, there were still Muslims who felt that a grave injustice had been done to Ali and to his family and they continued to support his memory. Moreover, they wanted Husayn, Ali's son, to become caliph. In 680 CE, however, soldiers who were supporters of the Umayyads killed Husayn. Shi'ite Muslims have always continued to hold Ali in the highest esteem and, in fact, believe that Muhammad personally wished that Ali would succeed him.

Among Shi'ite Muslims themselves there are some differences in views about subsequent leadership, and this has led to the development of subgroups. The different Shi'ite groups certainly all agree that the leader of the Muslim community should be a person who is descended from Ali and they use the term *imam* for such a leader. Differences between the Shi'ite groups tend to revolve around disputes concerning the holder of the title of imam at different periods. Many Muslims, for example, gave their support to Muhammad al-Baqir, who was a grandson of Husayn, to be the fifth imam. One group, however, gave their support to Zayd, who was the brother of Muhammad al-Baqir. Differences of opinion about who should be the seventh imam resulted in the subdivision of a group that became known as the Ismailis. They were influential in the founding of a dynasty called the Fatimids and also in the establishment of the university of Al-Azhar in Cairo. Ultimately, the Ismailis also evolved a number of specific beliefs which to some extent separated them from the mainstream belief system of the majority of Muslims. Another group of Shi'ites, known often as 'the twelvers', believe that the twelfth imam disappeared, but will return at some distant time in the future.

To return to the issue of the succession to Muhammad, the so-called Sunni Muslims, who are in the majority in the Muslim world, have a different view from the Shi'ites concerning the first three caliphs. They feel that Abu Bakr, the first caliph, was not ambitious to be caliph, but felt a responsibility to try to give some cohesion to the growing Muslim community. It is probably generally felt that, in any case, Ali was perhaps rather young to have been caliph at that time. In general, Sunni Muslims would probably feel that what happened in terms of the succession to Muhammad was reasonable. In any case, they would want to point out that as Muhammad was the 'Seal of the Prophets', it would not be possible for anyone to 'succeed' him in a spiritual sense, but only in terms of a leadership function within the Muslim community. The Sunni position is that this main branch of Islam represents the traditional view of Islam and reflects as far as it is possible to say the values and belief system as passed on in the revelations of Muhammad.

An important feature of the Islamic way of life is Islamic law, or the *Sharia*. This defines not only the general ethical principles but also some of the detailed aspects of the ways in which Muslims should conduct their lives. When Muhammad was alive, the Muslim community looked to him as an example and wherever possible followed his lifestyle and pattern of living. Even in the years following the death of Muhammad, people who had either known him or heard of the way he behaved were able to draw on this knowledge to sustain them and to help them decide how to handle difficult situations when they arose. They could always imagine how Muhammad might have behaved in a similar situation. The first four caliphs could be called upon for advice and would, if necessary, provide a judgement based on the decision they presumed Muhammad would have taken in a similar situation.

Gradually, however, as more and more time passed following Muhammad's death, it became increasingly difficult for people to rely with any certainty on how they thought Muhammad might have acted. It eventually became necessary to establish a system of Islamic law which would define appropriate behaviour in all kinds of situations. Jurisprudence is the study and analysis of the bases on which one might formulate laws, and Islamic jurisprudence came to be a very important area of study.

As Islamic law started to evolve, it developed slightly differently in different countries and cultures. One society gave emphasis to one aspect, another society to a different aspect. This was not very satisfactory, because, for example, an alleged transgression was viewed differently in those two different societies. Gradually people realized that one of the potential strengths of Islamic law was that the whole of Islamic society could be integrated by a system of law that was consistent for all. One of the leading scholars and thinkers

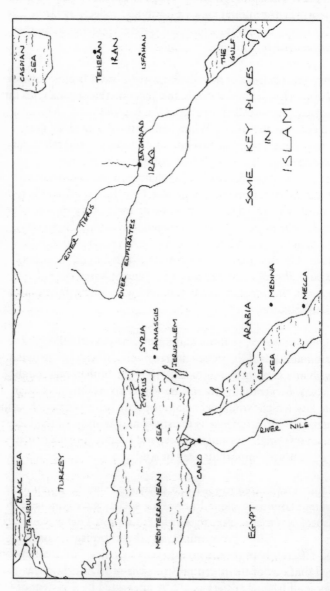

Figure 7.1 Some key places in Islam.

within the field of jurisprudence was al-Shafii, who was born in the eighth century CE. He was a leading advocate of the principle of uniformity of practice and suggested that there were four basic methods by which one could establish a law.

The first was by reference to the revelations in the Qur'an. The holy book, however, tended to provide guidance on general moral and religious issues and less on specific issues that might arise in the lives of people. One might think of the Qur'an, then, as the ultimate source of law, but there were other areas which also were helpful, according to al-Shafii. As mentioned earlier, the actual behaviour of Muhammad as a role model was very important; but by this period people were reliant on written accounts of his lifestyle. Muhammad's way of living and the manner in which he responded to different situations in his life are known as the *sunna*. These actions and responses are preserved in accounts known as *hadith*. Not all hadith are treated by Muslims as possessing the same validity and reliability. Muslim scholars have developed complex systems of reassuring themselves about the accuracy of hadith by methods which largely involve checking the means of transmission through the generations from Muhammad.

The third technique advocated by al-Shafii was that of reasoning by analogy. If a problematic situation arose which had not occurred before and Muslim scholars were not sure how to react to it in Islamic terms, they started by seeking an analogy. In other words, they tried to think of a situation that was similar to the new one in a number of ways and for which there was an established Islamic response. If it was agreed that there was sufficient commonality between the two situations, the decision applied to the earlier situation was adapted as appropriate to the new one. Finally, the fourth basis upon which one might derive laws was felt to be the consensus of the Muslim community. One can discern the principle of the idea here, but it became problematic whether one was thinking about the entire Muslim community or perhaps only a select group of scholars of jurisprudence. A gradual tendency became established for the latter to be the case.

10 THINGS TO REMEMBER

1 *Islam developed as a religion in Arabia in the seventh century* CE.

2 *The prophet Muhammad received a series of spiritual revelations from God, which form the basis of Islamic teaching.*

3 *Muhammad was born in Mecca in 570* CE.

4 *Muhammad married Khadija when he was about 25 years old.*

5 *Muhammad experienced his first religious revelation when he was about 40.*

6 *The subsequent series of revelations were enshrined in the Qur'an, which is the holy book of Muslims.*

7 *It was made clear by Muhammad that he was not the originator of the revelations, but that he was a vehicle for the transmission of God's message.*

8 *As a result of some persecution of Muhammad and his followers in Mecca, plans were made for a migration to Yathrib (Medina).*

9 *The migration, known as the Hijra, was completed in 622* CE.

10 *The Five Pillars are the five main duties that Muslims are expected to fulfil. These are the Profession of Faith, or* Shahada; *ritual prayer, or* salat; *the giving of alms, or* zakat; *fasting during* Ramadan; *and the* Hajj, *or pilgrimage to Mecca.*

8

The Baha'i faith

In this chapter you will learn about:
- *the history and development of the Baha'i faith*
- *the belief system of the faith*
- *the organization and administration of the Baha'i faith.*

History

The Baha'i faith evolved originally from another religion distinct from but related to Islam and was developed by a man named Sayyid Ali Muhammad, known perhaps more frequently as the Bab. He was born in Iran at Shiraz in 1819. The Bab was brought up within the Shi'ite tradition of Islam and gradually developed a reputation for being a devout and religiously-minded individual. As part of his general religious teaching, he began to suggest that he was destined to act on behalf of the 12th imam of Shia Islam, in terms of passing on his teachings to Muslims. This idea was in fact the derivation of the term Bab which means 'gate'. The Bab was viewed by many people as the gate through which Muslims could receive the teaching. It appears that in the mid-nineteenth century, the Bab was indeed considered by many people as a major religious figure and held in high esteem. Nevertheless, whenever in any religion a person lays claim to being able to act as any form of communication link for faith or teaching, there is the possibility that this will alienate some people. It appears that this is what happened in this case and that some established religious figures became rather suspicious of the Bab's activities.

With his growing number of religious followers, there also developed an increasing degree of political power. In the late 1840s, in spite of an increasing amount of criticism in some quarters, the Bab extended his spiritual claims. He claimed that he was actually the 12th imam who had returned. Although he was imprisoned by the authorities, he refused to recant and indeed went on to claim further that he was actually a manifestation of the divine. Given the social and religious context of the time, it was reasonably likely that such teachings would arouse the strong disapproval of the established religious order and this is exactly what happened. Meetings between followers of the Bab and of the more traditional elements in society often resulted in violence. In the context of the resultant destabilization, the political authorities acted and the Bab was executed at the town of Tabriz in 1850. The Bab wrote a great deal during his lifetime, including the *Bayan*, which contained spiritual revelations, discussions based upon the Qur'an and also analyses of religious theory.

Following the execution of the Bab, members of the religion were still persecuted to the extent that the religion only existed as a coherent movement within small isolated groups of adherents. However, a new leader did emerge, who was destined to lead members of the faith in a new direction. This leader was Mirza Husayn Ali Nuri, who became known as Baha'ullah. He was born in 1817 and became a member of the Bab faith in 1844. Those in authority in Iran had no desire, however, that another leader would emerge to replace the Bab and decided to exile Baha'ullah. He then found refuge in Iraq, from where he was permitted to act as a leader and inspiration to the few Babis living in Iran. It was during this period of his life that he also spent some time in the company of Sufi mystics.

Insight

The early members of the faith were clearly people of considerable conviction and determination, since such qualities were required to sustain the faith during periods of extensive persecution.

Although the Iraqis had generally supported Baha'ullah, eventually, in 1863, the Ottomans forced him to leave and he moved to Turkey. It was there that a new religion was founded, albeit one that drew a good deal upon the Bab's teachings. The new religion was called the Baha'i faith and it attracted many previous followers of the Bab. Although there were a number of doctrinal similarities between the Bab faith and the Baha'i faith, an important feature of the latter was that its adherents did not wish to become politically active. Another characteristic feature of the Baha'i faith was that it was conceived as being potentially a religion for the entire world and one that could attract converts from other faiths. Eventually Baha'ullah was expelled from Turkey and decided to settle in Syria. It was here that he died in 1892.

Following Baha'ullah's death, his eldest son assumed the leadership of the movement. He was known as Abdul Baha or Abbas Effendi. He was a very effective leader of the Baha'is and was instrumental in the establishment of groups of Baha'is in Western countries. He initiated a good deal of proselytizing since he believed with conviction that the faith was appropriate for people all over the world, in many different cultures. It was under the leadership of Abdul Baha that the focus of the Baha'i faith was moved from Akka in Syria to Haifa. Abdul Baha also travelled a great deal in the furtherance of the faith. He was in Egypt in 1910, and then in 1911 he visited communities of Baha'is in Paris and London.

Upon his death in 1921, he was succeeded by Shoghi Effendi. The latter was then 24 years of age and was the eldest of the grandchildren of Abdul Baha. Shoghi Effendi brought a rather new perspective to the faith, deriving partly from his Western education at Oxford. The many initiatives which he developed included a rapid programme for publishing works on the Baha'i faith, which was also an element in the general proselytizing approach of the faith. The administrative systems supporting the Baha'i faith were refined and made more efficient and an image was projected of a faith that was growing rapidly and was part of the modern world.

Shoghi Effendi was known among Baha'is as the Guardian of the Cause of God. He died in 1957.

Belief system

The Baha'i faith is a monotheistic faith and although Baha'is assert that God, as transcendent being, ultimately cannot be comprehended, they do feel that He is revealed to humanity by certain people at certain times in history. In particular, they regard certain people as 'manifestations of God'. Examples of such people have been Abraham, Muhammad, the Bab and Baha'ullah. The Baha'is suggest that all the main religions of the world share certain basic commonalities and as such we may regard all world faiths as being an expression of the same divine spirit. They claim that currently the Baha'i faith is the best available expression of that shared religious reality.

Insight

The Baha'i faith has a reputation for religious tolerance, and for respecting all the world's main religions. Baha'is view all the main faiths as exhibiting elements of religious truth.

Throughout the Baha'i faith, there is a sense of the universal nature of humanity. Human beings are seen to share certain rights and qualities as part of their shared humanity. This is another facet of the assertion that human beings also share a common spiritual tradition which transcends the specific practices of individual religions. There is a very strong emphasis on the equality of all human beings. Perhaps it is partly for this reason that the Baha'i faith does not have priests or people of equivalent status, as is the custom in a number of other religions. Again, perhaps partly because of the emphasis upon the equality of human beings, there is also great support among Baha'is for the world peace movement. Baha'is have been very supportive of international initiatives in such areas as human rights and environmental issues.

Baha'is attach great importance to the qualities of clear, rational thought and support the notion that each individual should not passively accept religious doctrine, but should investigate ideas for himself or herself. This emphasis upon rationality does not prevent Baha'is from pointing out that material existence is inadequate in terms of providing a high-quality life for people. The spiritual realm is also essential to having a balanced existence.

As scriptural texts, Baha'is attach a great deal of significance to the writings of Baha'ullah. These are considered to represent the spirit of God, and to be central to the faith. Examples of Baha'ullah's works include *Hidden Words* and the *Book of Certitude*.

Organization

During the time when Shoghi Effendi was the spiritual head of the faith, considerable advances were made in the way in which the faith was organized and managed. There was a developing system of groups which were linked together on a national and international basis through a well-organized and integrated management system. A system of education was developed for the faith, whereby its basic tenets could be disseminated among, for example, new members. A formal system of membership was also introduced for the faith. Over the last half century there has been an extensive programme of establishing buildings as a focus for worship and establishing contacts with international organizations.

After the death of Shoghi Effendi it was determined that there would no longer be a single person who was regarded as the leader of the faith. In place of a single leader there was to be an elected body called the House of Justice, which would take decisions collectively. The Universal House of Justice first assumed leadership of the approximately five million Baha'is in 1963. The constitution of the House of Justice is that nine representatives are elected at five-year intervals.

Insight

The idea of collective and democratic leadership, avoiding having a single decision-maker, appears to be in keeping with the spirit of equality and tolerance characteristic of the Baha'i movement.

In its spiritual practice and ritual the Baha'i faith owes much to its cultural and historical roots in Islam, to the extent that practices include ritual prayer; ritual fasting once a year; and making a pilgrimage. When Baha'is pray they do so in a specific direction, but this is that of the tomb of Baha'ullah, located in Israel. Baha'is have their own specific places of pilgrimage, which are usually either the former house of the Bab in Iran or Baha'ullah's former home in Iraq. Baha'is do not practise a great deal of formality when it comes to worship and this usually takes place in the house of a member or in another unostentatious building. This is perhaps in keeping with the philosophy of the equality of all human beings which has been so strongly espoused by Baha'is.

10 THINGS TO REMEMBER

1 *The Baha'i faith developed out of the religious teaching of Sayyid Ali Muhammad.*

2 *He was born in Iran in 1819 and known as the Bab.*

3 *The Bab was executed in 1850.*

4 *A new leader named Mirza Husayn Ali Nuri (also known as Baha'ullah) assumed the role of the Bab.*

5 *The Iranian authorities exiled Baha'ullah.*

6 *He lived in Iraq, then Turkey and finally Syria, where he died in 1892.*

7 *Baha'ullah founded the new religion of the Baha'i faith, which was intended to become a religion for the whole world.*

8 *Abbas Effendi, the son of Baha'ullah, took over the leadership of the movement from his father.*

9 *Abbas Effendi did much to advance the cause of the faith in the West.*

10 *On his death in 1921, he was succeeded by Shoghi Effendi.*

9

Hinduism

In this chapter you will learn about:
- *key Hindu texts and the teachings they contain*
- *the Hindu way of life*
- *religious practice in the home and at the Hindu temple.*

History

Hinduism is the ancient religion of India. Although it has spread to a limited extent outside the Indian subcontinent, and has also been carried by Hindu families as migrants to most parts of the world, it still remains a distinctively Indian phenomenon. It is not a revealed religion, in the sense that a single person outlined its belief system. Rather, it is more accurate to see it as a process of accretion and evolution. While Hinduism has many different gods and goddesses, it may also quite reasonably be viewed as a monotheistic religion, in the sense of the belief in an all-encompassing spiritual force in the universe. The faith possesses a strong mystical element, and has perhaps a wider range of doctrines and devotional practices than any other religion. This diversity makes it difficult to summarize Hinduism. However, it is perhaps this very diversity coupled with flexibility that has enabled Hinduism to survive for between three and four millennia, even during periods when India has been ruled by external countries.

Insight

As a religion, Hinduism has been very flexible in terms of absorbing ideas from other faiths. This has tended to help avoid confrontation between Hinduism and other religions, thus helping to preserve the Hindu faith.

The origins of Hinduism can be conveniently traced back to about the beginning of the second millennium BCE. At this time there was a large population of nomadic people living in the central Asian steppes. They herded grazing animals and engaged in agriculture to a limited degree. At this point in history, these people started to migrate outwards from the steppes. Some groups moved eastwards and some westwards. Others moved south and invaded India. It is difficult to be sure what motivated these mass migrations. It could have been climatic changes or it could have been a lack of grazing pastures. These migrating people were known as Aryans. They had fast-moving chariots and were a fairly warlike people. Although one may assume that the indigenous inhabitants of northern India attempted to repulse the invaders, the Aryans quickly became established as the ruling authority.

One characteristic feature of the Aryans was that within their society there existed an influential group of priests who recited hymns to the gods and performed the appropriate sacrifices. These priests were known as *brahmins*, and the collection of hymns they used was termed the *Rig Veda*. Originally, this was passed on orally from generation to generation of brahmins, but eventually it was written down in Sanskrit, and exists today as one of the oldest of scriptures. The brahmin social class attained considerable power and authority in ancient India, and this has to some extent continued into modern India. The social power of the brahmins resided in the fact that they were able to offer the correct sacrifices to the gods and hence ensure divine intervention in favour of society. Without their knowledge of the appropriate hymns and prayers, there was fear that disaster could befall society. Many brahmins led very devout lives, being attached to temples or living as recluses in the forest. Others, however, led secular lives, working in administration or in the service of the ruler.

The brahmins were at the top of the social hierarchy and below them in the social system were three other social strata or *varnas*. These were, in order of status, the *kshatriyas*, the *vaishyas*, and the *shudras*. The kshatriyas were originally the warrior caste, whose function was to defend the kingdom. The vaishyas were tradespeople, merchants, farmers and craftsmen in metals. Their participation in commerce ensured that successful traders could potentially become very wealthy. These first three social castes were all considered to be true Aryans and were termed the 'twice-born'. This signified that, in addition to their natural birth, they underwent an initiation in puberty when a sacred thread was draped about their shoulders. The fourth social grouping, the shudras, were not twice-born and were essentially low-status peasants and serfs. Their role was to support the members of the other three classes. In addition, as non-Aryans, they were not allowed to hear the recitation of the *Vedas*. Although the four social classes were conceived of as fairly rigid divisions, there was a limited degree of social mobility. Over a period of time, perhaps several generations, a family or families of vaishyas may have become rich through business and commerce and succeeded in redefining themselves within a higher-status social grouping. This was certainly not the norm, although it was possible for it to happen.

Insight

The Hindu caste system is conceived by some as dysfunctional through its rigidity, and because it appears to encourage some people to remain within a fixed social band. On the other hand, it can be said to provide a sense of place for people, and a degree of cohesion in society.

Outside the four main social classes were the untouchables or 'outcastes'. Normally this group carried out jobs that were regarded as ritually polluting for the higher classes. They would often be required to live outside the village boundaries, in order that the other four social classes would not have to come into contact with them.

The *Rig Veda* contains over 1,000 hymns and evolved during the period from about 1500 BCE to 1000 BCE. There are other vedic texts that were associated with the *Rig Veda*, but generally not considered as important historically. The recitation of the vedic hymns and the performance by the brahmins of the appropriate sacrifices enabled the Aryans to seek the assistance of the gods in their daily lives. The gods of the *Rig Veda* included Indra, who was the god of war and of storms; Agni, the god of fire, who was important in the temple sacrifices; Varuna, the creator god; and Savitar, the god of the sun. During the sacrifices to the gods, it is recorded that the Aryans consumed a drink called *soma*, which helped them to have divine visions. The drink was prepared from herbal sources and almost certainly contained a narcotic of some kind. There are supplementary texts at the end of the Vedas, termed the *Brahmanas* and the Upanishads. The former are lengthy texts which were produced between about 800 BCE and 500 BCE and they contain, among other things, instructions for the conduct of religious ceremonies. The Upanishads date from about 600 BCE onwards and are mystical texts written by Hindu sages. They speak of the ideal of the reclusive, ascetic, meditative life and of the individual who seeks to unite the human soul with that of the all-pervading spiritual force of the universe – *Brahman*. It was also during the upanishadic period that the doctrine of reincarnation developed, along with the notion that it was in principle possible for the individual soul to escape from the wheel of reincarnation and attain *moksha*, or spiritual release.

From about 100 BCE onwards, a school of Hindu philosophy called *vedanta* developed. The principal texts of vedanta were the *Brahma Sutras* and the Upanishads. Vedanta is to this day one of the principal sources of inspiration for modern philosophical Hinduism. Arguably vedanta's most famous exponent and advocate was the philosopher and mystic called Sankara, who lived (very approximately) from 789 to 830 CE. Sankara was born in southern India and argued that salvation for the individual could best be gained through knowledge, or *jnana*. The philosophical system which he founded is often known as non-dualism, or *advaita*, because it proposes that the human soul and the divine soul or Brahman are essentially one and the same. Brahman, the all-pervading power of the universe, is argued to be the only ultimate reality. As a practical method Sankara advised religious aspirants to engage in meditation, through which they would enable the individual soul to become one with Brahman, and hence gain salvation.

From approximately medieval times in India, there was an increasing movement away from the rather philosophical system of Sankara, to religious practices involving devotion to a more personal god. Ramanuja, who lived from about 1050 to 1137 CE, was an important representative of this so-called *bhakti* or devotional school. Ramanuja did not demur from the essentials of the system of non-duality, but suggested that there were some differences between the substance of the individual soul and that of Brahman. Hence the notion of the individual human being worshipping an immanent god became possible. Under such a system the salvation of the individual depended on the level of devotion demonstrated by the devotee and also on the grace of God. There were many other schools of thought, however, within the broad area of Hinduism. In the thirteenth century, for instance, Madhva argued for the philosophy of dualism, which suggested that the human soul and the divine soul were entirely separate.

During the last few centuries new movements and tendencies have developed in Hinduism, often partly because of the influence of other nations and peoples, during, for example, the Mughal dynasties and the British rule of India. Ram Mohan Roy (1772–1833) was very much influenced by the rationalism of the British and had less regard for some of the more esoteric practices and traditions of Hinduism. He was, for example, very much against the worship of images of the Hindu gods and he also mounted a very successful campaign against the practice of *sati*, or the self-immolation of widows on the funeral pyres of their husbands. In 1828 he founded an organization called the *Brahmo Samaj*, which was devoted in part to the systematic study of religion.

In 1875 Madame Blavatsky founded the Theosophical Society in the United States and later moved to India. This society did a great deal to publicize Hinduism beyond the shores of India and to some extent make its principles available to Westerners, rather than purely for Hindus. Other influential Hindus of the modern era include Ramakrishna, a Bengali saint and mystic who argued for the essential unity of all religions. One of his disciples, Vivekananda, attended the World Parliament of Religions in Chicago in 1893 and besides bringing Hinduism to the attention of the West once more, he advocated a synthesis of Western and Hindu thought and philosophy.

Of all modern Hindus, M.K. Gandhi is arguably the most famous. The Bengali poet Rabindranath Tagore called Gandhi *Mahatma*, or great soul, a name which remained with Gandhi during his lifetime and afterwards. Born in Porbander in 1869, Gandhi was not an outstanding student and was sent eventually to London to train as a barrister. He worked first in South Africa where he developed a reputation as a lawyer and social activist, helping the Indian community to assert its legal and social rights. Upon returning to India, he became involved in the campaign for independence. He was a deeply devoted Hindu who tried to apply the teachings of the *Bhagavad Gita* in his everyday life and in politics. In his famous political protests he consistently applied the principles of non-violence which made him famous. Although he was in continuous opposition to British rule, on many occasions leading British administrators found that they respected him for the ethical manner in which he conducted himself. He was a lifelong advocate of vegetarianism. Gandhi inevitably made enemies in the complex political situation leading up to India's independence and he was assassinated by a Hindu radical who felt he had abandoned the traditional Hindu cause.

Insight

Gandhi was devoted to the scripture of the *Bhagavad Gita*, and in particular its philosophy that human beings should not act for themselves, but should carry out good works in the name of God.

Belief system

In Hinduism, religious beliefs and practice are inextricably linked with the social and cultural systems of India. Ritual and tradition play a very significant part in Indian life and affect many of the stages of individual existence. The life of the Hindu was, and is, considered to fall, ideally, into four main stages or *ashramas* – the first being that of religious student. This stage began when at puberty the Hindu boy was invested with the *yajnopavita*, or sacred thread. This ceremony, called the *upanayana*, or second birth, marked the transition from childhood to the student stage. The boy became a *brahmacharin*, or student of the Vedas, under the supervision of a guru, who would introduce him to the teachings of the Vedas. The sacred thread was a loop made of white cotton and was placed over the right shoulder and under the left armpit. From then on it was supposed to remain with the young man for life. The *upanayana* ceremony was regarded as having deep significance and at it was chanted a holy *mantram* from the *Rig Veda*. This is called the *Gayatri Mantram* and is still recited by devout Hindus today. Although the sacred thread ceremony was largely for boys, girls were also sometimes initiated.

The second *ashrama* is the family stage, or *grhastha*. Having studied under his guru for several years, the young man becomes married and assumes family responsibilities. This stage continues throughout the middle age of the man, while his and his wife's children grow and eventually get married themselves. At about this time the man leaves the family home and breaks most ties with his family. He becomes a recluse in a remote area, lives in a small hut, and meditates. This is the third, *vanaprastha* stage.

Finally, the by now elderly man leaves his simple home and becomes a wandering mendicant or *sannyasin*. From now on he will visit holy places and make pilgrimages. He will beg for alms and lead this wandering life until he dies.

By no means all men led or lead this pattern of life. It is regarded as an 'ideal type' of life to which one might aspire, but which in reality may not take place for many people. For many, the family stage may continue for the remainder of life, with the man spending short periods in a monastery or on pilgrimages to holy places. Equally well, there is a long tradition in India of young men becoming itinerant monks or *sadhus* and spending their whole life in this way. Although many aspects of this traditional patterning of life are orientated towards the male gender, some women also adopt the wandering holy life. As in most societies, it is probably true to say that in India there is every combination of lifestyle, and way of structuring the life of the individual. The *ashramas*, however, have the function of embedding the notions of the religious student, the family person and the religious recluse within the concept of how one might ideally conduct one's life.

Insight

The many *sadhus* leading an itinerant spiritual life in India are to some extent seen as an anachronism in a country which is rapidly developing technologically and scientifically.

Among all the Hindu scriptures, the Upanishads have arguably had the greatest influence upon the mystical elements in Hinduism. The word *upanishad* means something approximating to 'sitting close alongside'. It reflects the notion that the mystical teaching of the Upanishads was transmitted typically from guru to student in a close, personal teaching situation. The Upanishads are the concluding section of the Vedas, and deal not with the procedures for ceremonies, but with the mystical awareness of the divine. The authors of the Upanishads are unknown, but it is a reasonable assumption that they were wandering mystics who wished to transmit their own religious experiences. This experience was not based on a strict, regimented study of the scriptures, but on meditation and a direct contemplation of God. There are 108 Upanishads, and far more may have existed but been lost. Each is different in form and style, but there are recurring themes. The principal theme is the relationship between Brahman, the divine spiritual force of the universe, and the soul of the individual human being. Brahman exists in the human soul and if only human beings can recognize that presence and understand the significance of this, then they will no longer be subject to the eternal round of birth and death. Each Upanishad emphasizes a different element of this broad theme.

The *Katha Upanishad* describes the entire universe as coming from Brahman. Each individual human being has a lifetime in which to comprehend Brahman and to join with Brahman. If this is not achieved before the person dies, then s/he must be reincarnated and have another opportunity to understand the divine spirit. Brahman cannot be seen or touched, but exists in each and every soul and the presence can be revealed through meditation. The purpose of meditation is to calm the senses so that they are not disturbed by changes in the environment, however severe. Meditation also seeks to develop a tranquil mind, uncluttered by disturbing thoughts. The attainment of such a psychological state is termed *yoga*. Its ultimate purpose is to attain an understanding of Brahman existing in the soul, a situation described as the real or true self. In addition to this true self, the individual exists in the phenomenal world of everyday events. This is an impermanent world, in contrast to the eternal soul united with Brahman.

In the *Isha Upanishad*, the everyday life of the world is described again as being fundamentally imperfect. It is very different from the knowledge that can be attained through the process of meditation. The *Isha Upanishad* stresses that where one is involved in the world, it is important to act but not to become attached to the fruits of the actions. One should act in a moral and ethical manner but should not wish for any particular outcome, especially one that would benefit oneself. In this way one becomes detached from the world, even though one acts within it. One has no desires for any particular outcome. This is one way, argues the *Isha Upanishad*, in which a human being can attain union with Brahman and hence release from the round of birth and death.

The *Chandogya Upanishad* speaks of the impermanence of the empirical world. We realize in an intellectual sense that life must end, but we often do not let that knowledge affect the way in which we live our everyday lives. We continue to seek wealth and possessions, knowing that ultimately we will leave them. This Upanishad argues that the only way to gain true happiness is to seek to know Brahman. The *Brihadaranyaka Upanishad* repeats the theme that it is very difficult to gain liberation from rebirth and yet the way to achieve this is to understand that the human soul and Brahman are one.

The messages of the *Kaivalya Upanishad* and the *Svetasvatara Upanishad* are very similar. They provide practical techniques for knowing Brahman. One should have confidence in one's guru to provide the correct guidance and teaching. The aspirant should then locate a quiet and peaceful place in which to meditate upon Brahman. One should sit in the posture of a yogi and try to calm the mind and the senses. A devotion to such meditative practices will encourage the individual to relinquish desires for material things and to see that the soul united with Brahman is immortal.

The concept of salvation was central to the discussions that took place in the Upanishads and it was during this period that the notion of *karma* started to develop. Karma is a rather general word that can signify a number of related concepts. It may mean the work that human beings carry out, the actions they perform or the way in which they respond in terms of behaviour to other human beings. The notion of karma is, however, inextricably linked with Hindu ethics and with salvation. The central idea of karma is that if human beings behave unethically, they cannot avoid the consequences of their actions. The unethical actions will be certain to have undesirable consequences for those human beings in the future. There is, according to the doctrine, no escaping the consequences of karma. There is a clear, logical link between unethical actions and the undesirable results. One might feel that this doctrine suggests that there is little purpose in making an effort in life, since one is, in a sense, a victim of one's past unsatisfactory actions. Nevertheless, it is considered that one should still strive to behave morally, since this will gradually reduce karma associated with the human soul. Eventually this will result in the elimination of all karma and the individual soul will no longer be reborn and will achieve salvation.

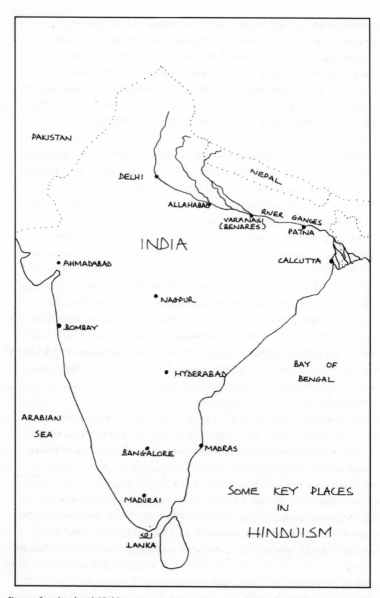

PAKISTAN

DELHI

NEPAL

ALLAHABAD

VARANASI
(BENARES)

RIVER GANGES

PATNA

INDIA

AHMADABAD

CALCUTTA

NAGPUR

BOMBAY

HYDERABAD

BAY OF
BENGAL

ARABIAN
SEA

BANGALORE

MADRAS

SOME KEY PLACES
IN
HINDUISM

MADURAI

SRI
LANKA

Figure 9.1 Some key places in Hinduism.

Unless karma can be gradually reduced, the human soul will continue to be reborn time and time again. This process of transmigration or continual rebirth is sometimes referred to as *samsara*. The Hindu assumes that a diligent attempt to behave morally will eventually result in the dissolution of karma and the soul will achieve salvation or release from samsara. The release from transmigration is often referred to as *moksha*.

Hinduism has evolved a number of different strategies for trying to achieve salvation and perhaps the best known of these is yoga. *Hatha yoga* has become very popular in the West because of the variety of postures incorporated in the discipline and its use as a form of physical exercise and relaxation. However, there is much more to the study and practice of yoga than the postures, or *asanas*. The word *yoga* is derived from the same root as the word 'yoke', and the latter word suggests the joining together of the individual soul and the universal soul of Brahman. Although the word yoga is generally used, particularly in the West, to refer to yoga postures, it is actually one of the major historical philosophical traditions of Hinduism. There are numerous texts and writings on yoga, although arguably the definitive source is the *Yoga Sutras* written by Patanjali in about the first century CE.

Insight

Arguably unlike any other country, India is preoccupied with religion and with the idea of attaining a sense of union with God. Various forms of meditation and yoga are widely practised to this end.

The discipline of yoga consists of a wide variety of practices. Students of yoga are expected to behave morally and to conform to the traditions of non-violence, of telling the truth and of generosity, of abstaining from sexual behaviour and of not taking the possessions of others. Second, they are expected to practise the range of asanas, and the exercises that result in the control of the breath (*pranayama*). Finally they should practise calming the mind through meditation (*dhyana*), which will lead, according to yoga adepts, to the state of *samadhi* involving total peace and union of the human soul with the universal soul. There is a great deal of reliable observational evidence that Indian yogis have developed unusual powers through their spiritual disciplines. This, however, is not really the true purpose of yoga, which is centrally concerned with the attainment of salvation and release from the cycle of samsara.

One of the best-known and most widely read scriptures of Hinduism is the *Bhagavad Gita*. This is a relatively short book of 18 chapters which is part of the long Hindu epic, the *Mahabharata*. It is difficult to date the origin of the *Bhagavad Gita*, but it was probably created in about 300 BCE. At the opening of the *Gita*, two great armies face each other across the battlefield. Arjuna is a leader of one of the armies and he commands his charioteer to drive him out between the armies so that he can survey them. When he does so, he is aghast that there are so many relatives and family members facing each other. He feels that it would almost be better if he were not to resist and were killed by the opposing army. Arjuna becomes utterly despondent and does not really want to fight.

However, Arjuna's charioteer is none other than the deity Krishna and this situation in which Arjuna finds himself provides a medium for Krishna to deliver an analysis of the nature of life and death and the dilemmas in which human beings find themselves. Krishna says to Arjuna that he should lift himself psychologically and not be downcast. Krishna starts by arguing that the soul cannot be killed. The human body may die or be killed but the soul lives on for ever. Krishna is thus suggesting that there exists the material world which has a finite end, but that there is also the world of the soul which is not limited in this way. Arjuna is thus advised to fight, for if he does not fight, he will lose his honour. It is a debatable question whether the dilemma of the *Bhagavad Gita* refers to a real battle or whether the battle is merely a metaphor for the human condition and the moral battles that humans must fight throughout their lives. Whatever the historical truth, this situation provides a context within which Krishna can discuss the spiritual nature of humanity.

Krishna then embarks on one of the principal messages of the *Gita*. This is that people should engage with the world and do their work and duty, yet not become attached to the possible consequences of that work. If one works because one desires a certain outcome, then one's equanimity is disturbed and one cannot work with peace of mind. Human beings can very easily be attracted to the material world and to possessions. This, argues Krishna, only brings unhappiness. If one becomes too attached to the self and to the desires to satisfy the self, this ultimately brings unhappiness. The true spiritual way is to abandon attachment to the senses, and to concentrate on trying to achieve a state of equanimity and peace which is undisturbed by attraction to the material world.

The true yogi, argues Krishna, always tries to benefit the rest of humanity. S/he acts in an unselfish manner in order to try to do good. Equally, the true yogi dedicates all actions to God and attempts to act in a manner which would be pleasing to God. The religious person tries to strike a balance between extremes in all things and does not act out of a motive of selfishness. The yogi tries to avoid all preoccupation with the self and with trying to achieve something because it will provide the individual with a sense of self-satisfaction. The entire purpose of karma yoga or of unselfish action is to act in such a manner that the result will benefit others.

Organization

Religious practice in Hinduism may, on the one hand, be highly organized but, on the other, it may be very devolved to the level of the individual practitioner. There are large temples with priests administering and officiating, and there are many individual holy men who interpret the scriptures and tradition in their own way and develop and teach their own variant of religious practice. It is also worth noting that the family home is a very significant place of worship and religious practice, and many people may visit the temple only intermittently.

Most families will have a shrine within the home. This may be on a shelf on the wall or set in a niche in a corner. It could also be a rather grander affair set up on a table. There would typically be small statues of gods and goddesses such as Krishna, Radha or Ganesh. Colourful paintings of deities or religious scenes might also be present. There may be some holy verses such as the *Gayatri Mantram* and the whole would be decorated in a very ornate manner with tinsel, gold paint or whatever else could be used. In the family home the shrine may be used to keep photographs of deceased relatives on display and regular prayers will be said for them. When family members come into the home they may walk up to the shrine and say a few short prayers and similarly just as they are leaving the home. Family members may also emulate the common practice in the temple, of leaving items of fruit or sweets as an offering before the statues of the gods.

In a Hindu temple there will usually be several statues of gods and goddesses, depending, to some extent, on the size of the temple. Within the temple there will usually be several smaller shrines set into the wall, as well as the main shrine at the (usually) western end of the temple. The temple is regarded as the home of the deity and the latter is treated in many ways like a human being. In the early morning, the statue of the deity is washed and dressed, and offerings of fruit and flowers are placed before the statue. The temple priest will say prayers and chant hymns in a ceremony normally described by the general term of *puja*. Temple priests are trained in the Vedas and in the hymns and religious ceremonies and are mainly concerned with the administration of the temple and the performance of the necessary religious functions. The role of the spiritual teacher, however, is taken by the guru, who may not be attached to a conventional temple. It is more likely that the guru will have established an *ashram* or monastery where people may go to receive practical spiritual guidance or instruction in meditation or yoga.

Many temples also function as community centres. People attend them as a social centre, as well as a place of worship. Much religious devotion and ceremony take place in the home, but people will also attend the temple for congregational worship and to receive *darshan* or grace from the deity. In general, it is probably reasonable to argue that Hinduism does not have the same degree of uniform organization as many religions. By contrast, the diversity of the system adds an enormous richness to Hindu practice.

In recent years, a number of Hindu organizations have been established in the West, and have attracted large numbers of followers. One of the best-known is the International Society for Krishna Consciousness (ISKCON). This was established in 1966 by Swami Prabhupada. As its name suggests, the organization regards Krishna as the symbol of the Divine, and the object of devotional prayer and chanting. To the extent that ISKCON sees there being a single divinity in the universe, it can be considered a monotheistic approach. The organization is part of a long, historic tradition in India, often known as the *bhakti*, or devotional movement. One of its characteristic practices is the extensive chanting of mantra employing the name of Krishna. In terms of scriptures, the *Bhagavad Gita* is perhaps the most important text within the organization. However, following the impetus of Swami Prabhupada, the organization has embarked upon an extensive programme of publishing scriptures and educational texts related to the broad teachings of the movement.

Perhaps it is the very diversity of Hinduism which at least partly explains the reasons for it becoming popular in the West. Devotees can select from a range of organizations, practices and teachings, which, while all subscribing to the broad principles of Hinduism, provide a basis for the spiritual inclinations of different individuals.

10 THINGS TO REMEMBER

1 *The origins of Hinduism can be traced back to the religion of the Aryan invaders of India in the second millennium* BCE.

2 *In ancient India there originated a system of social stratification known as the caste system.*

3 *There were four main castes, known as the* brahmins *or priests;* kshatriyas *or warriors;* vaishyas *or tradespeople; and* shudras *or workers.*

4 *There were also people outside the caste system known as 'untouchables' or 'outcastes'.*

5 *Elements of the caste system persist to this day.*

6 *One of the earliest scriptures of the Aryans was the* Rig Veda.

7 *Other important Hindu texts are the* Upanishads *which date from about 600* BCE.

8 *The word* upanishad *means approximately 'sitting close alongside' and reflects the role of the guru in passing on spiritual teachings.*

9 *The main theme of the Upanishads is the relationship between the universal soul, Brahman, and the souls of individual human beings.*

10 *On one level, Hinduism can be seen as monotheistic, with Brahman being the all-pervading power in the universe.*

10

Buddhism

In this chapter you will learn about:
- *the life and teachings of Siddhartha*
- *the different schools of Buddhism*
- *the Noble Eightfold Path of Buddhism.*

History

Buddhism is a faith, a world view, a way of living and a psychology. More particularly, it is a way of living which seeks to minimize and ultimately eliminate the kinds of thoughts and actions that cause human beings to suffer. Buddhism tends to rest on the argument that much suffering for human beings results from the nature of our reaction to events, rather than necessarily the nature of those events. It prescribes a set of strategies for dealing with the events and circumstances of life, in such a way that the consequences cause us less suffering. These practical strategies were developed by Siddhartha Gautama who was born in 563 BCE near Lumbini in what is now Nepal. Siddhartha's father was named Suddhodana, and was the king of the Sakya kingdom in the southern region of Nepal. Siddhartha died in about 486 BCE.

As a young man, Siddhartha lived in relatively affluent circumstances for the time. However, according to accounts of his life, he did not find this affluence particularly satisfying and felt that his destiny lay elsewhere. One day he encountered a very old and feeble man near his father's palace. This caused him to reflect upon the destiny of all human beings – that of growing old. This lesson in human destiny was reinforced when he subsequently came across a man who was badly diseased and then later again a dead person. The impact of this on the young Siddhartha was to cause him to reflect on the idea that, no matter how affluent his present lifestyle, ultimately he would die just like every other human being. He found this a very pessimistic idea, but he then encountered a fourth person – a wandering ascetic. Although the person had no possessions and lived a very simple life, he appeared to possess a form of happiness and a sense of equanimity which suggested to Siddhartha that there was a way of life within which one could find peace, even though the nature of human destiny seemed apparently unhappy.

Insight

Siddhartha had experienced his first understanding of the phenomenon of impermanence, the idea that all entities in the universe are destined eventually to disperse into their component parts.

Although he returned to the palace, Siddhartha was unable to forget his vision of the wandering ascetic. Eventually, he decided to make a break with conventional life and left the palace in secret, to become a *sadhu*, or wandering mendicant. He studied meditation and fasted frequently. At one point he joined a group of five other ascetics. They tended to look on Siddhartha as their leader because he was so strict in his own asceticism. Eventually, however, Siddhartha began to have doubts about the effectiveness of the mendicant lifestyle, and started to live in a less extreme way. One of the results of this was that the other ascetics left him, because they felt that he was not abiding by his principles.

Siddhartha decided to undergo a long period of meditation and selected a tree under which to sit. He determined that he would not cease meditating until he had understood the purpose of human existence and had developed a strategy to remove the causes of human suffering. After a long time in meditation Siddhartha achieved his goal and became enlightened. From then on he was known as the Buddha, or enlightened one. However, he faced an initial dilemma in wondering whether he would be able to explain his relatively profound philosophy to other people. He was concerned that he might not be able to teach it to others and hence it would be misunderstood. Ultimately, however, he decided to try to transmit the results of his enlightenment experience. He walked to the Deer Park just outside the city of Benares, and there delivered his first sermon, which expounded the essentials of his philosophical system. His audience consisted of the same five ascetics he had known before and they were so inspired by his teaching that they became his first disciples. Indeed, the Buddha ordained them as the first *bhikkhus*, or Buddhist monks, and they became the foundation of the *sangha*, or community of Buddhists. The Buddha also later initiated an order of nuns.

Towards the end of his life, at the age of about 80, the Buddha started to walk in the direction of Kusinagara. On the way he was a guest in a home in the town of Pava and there ate a meal of pork which is assumed not to have been fresh. Afterwards he developed dysentery and later died near the town of Kusinagara. The Buddha had refused to name a successor to lead the community. His view was that each individual person had to strive on their own to attain an understanding of the world and that the disciplines he had taught would provide the foundation on which this could be achieved. The Buddha considered that his teachings were at the heart of what he had contributed to humanity.

The Buddha's teaching was disseminated largely by the *sangha* of monks and nuns. They led the life of wandering mendicants, owning no possessions and begging each day for food alms. Their lifestyle was controlled by the *vinaya*, or monastic code. This had been specified by the Buddha and included such aspects as the means by which they were to obtain and eat their food. Most of the year the monks wandered from place to place, teaching and holding discussions with laypeople. However, during the rainy season, or *vassa*, there developed a tradition of residing in one place, where the monks were supported with food and accommodation by laypeople. Indeed, there was a gradual tendency for the monks and nuns to live in monasteries, or *viharas*. Some of these developed into very large communities of learning such as that at Nalanda.

After the Buddha's death there was an understandable tendency to wish to consolidate the teaching and agree it in a standard form. To this end it is generally considered that a series of councils was held. The first was held at Rajagrha, fairly soon after the death of the Buddha, and among other things helped to agree the form of the *vinaya*. The second council is supposed to have been held at Vaisali, while the third was sponsored by the emperor Asoka and held at Pataliputra. Asoka had been converted to Buddhism and provided the faith with considerable support. It was at this council that large numbers of Buddhist scriptures were agreed in the medium of Sanskrit.

Asoka was in some ways a unique ruler. He assumed his position as ruler of almost the entire Indian subcontinent in 268 BCE and was at first an authoritarian ruler comparable with the standards of the time. He invaded and subdued the region of Kalinga in about 260 BCE, with the death of many thousands of those conquered. The resultant suffering caused Asoka to reflect on his actions and he came to the conclusion that he should rule in a different manner. He converted to Buddhism and remained a Buddhist until his death in 239 BCE. Throughout the whole of this period he attempted to rule India according to Buddhist principles. As far as was practically possible he tried to be compassionate to his enemies and to use the minimum of violence. In different parts of India he set up stone columns, many of which still exist, on which are inscribed principles of Buddhist ethics to which Asoka declared he was trying to adhere. These stone columns remain a testament to a king who gave Buddhism enormous support and who also tried to rule a large and diverse country according to ethical principles.

From the relatively early days of Buddhism doctrinal divisions developed. These became more and more significant until it was possible to discern two clear branches of Buddhism. The *Theravada*, or Way of the Elders, was the school of Buddhism that developed in Sri Lanka and South-east Asia. It inherited its traditions from the early monks of the *sangha* and its religious texts consist of the canon in the Pali language. The *Mahayana*, or Great Vehicle, developed in Tibet, China and Japan. The Mahayana developed the concept of the *bodhisattva*, the individual who has the capacity to attain enlightenment but chooses to remain outside *nirvana* in order to assist others in obtaining enlightenment. Within Mahayana, Japanese Buddhism evolved in a distinctively different way, producing the Zen tradition. The underlying ideas of Zen (known in China as Ch'an) had been taken to China by the Indian monk Bodhidharma in the early sixth century CE. It is a form of Buddhism which places great emphasis upon meditation. A Buddhist tradition developed in Tibet from the seventh century onwards, which incorporated esoteric elements of tantrism within the mainstream Mahayana teachings.

In India, the country of its origin, Buddhism attained a good deal of support at first, but eventually declined. However, it became firmly established in other countries. It remained a faith of the East for many centuries and only within the last century or so has it become firmly established in the West. In 1881 the Pali Text Society was established by, among others, T.W. Rhys Davids and this organization has been extremely influential in translating the Pali Buddhist text into English. In 1924 the Buddhist Society was founded in England and this society has been at the forefront of disseminating Buddhist teachings in the West. Other very significant Buddhist centres developed, including the Samye Ling Tibetan Buddhist centre in Scotland and the San Francisco Zen Centre in the United States.

The Theravada tradition has become well established through the work of, among others, Ajahn Sumedho, an American who was ordained in Thailand in the 1960s and studied under Ajahn Chah. In 1979 the English Sangha Trust along with Ajahn Sumedho founded Chithurst Buddhist Monastery in southern England. This was followed later by Amaravati Buddhist Centre which was established north of London in 1984. Both Chithurst and Amaravati have become important centres for the teaching of Buddhist meditation according to the Theravada tradition.

Belief system

After the Buddha's enlightenment, he walked to the Deer Park at Sarnath near Benares, where he encountered the five *sadhus* he had known earlier in his life. At first they rejected him because they felt that he had abandoned his principles of asceticism and was leading too materialistic a life. However, they were gradually affected by his peaceful countenance and after a while felt more positively disposed towards him. The Buddha then preached to them the Sermon of the Turning of the Wheel of the Law, during which he enunciated the Four Noble Truths and the Noble Eightfold Path which were to form the core of Buddhist teachings. In essence the Buddha advocated a 'Middle Way' as the preferred route of spiritual practice, avoiding both excess asceticism and excess materialism.

Insight
The basic approach of the Middle Way was that monks and nuns should only consume food and use materials that were necessary for the maintenance of a healthy life. Luxuries were to be avoided.

The first Noble Truth and the starting point for the Buddha's analysis of the human condition is that suffering and sorrow exist in the world. Perhaps the most obvious form of suffering is that resulting from physical pain as a consequence of illness, infirmity or old age. There are certain inevitable results of the human condition such as death, which also cause us to suffer. In this case we tend to suffer when we contemplate death. We suffer because the notion of extinction of the body and mind is a disturbing idea. We normally do not wish our lives to end, and yet we know in our deepest thoughts that death is inevitable.

The Buddha also argued that a great deal of suffering is caused through the general unsatisfactory nature of the world. Our lives are rarely as we would really like them to be in a perfect world. We do not have as nice a car as we would really like; we might prefer to have a larger house with a drive of its own; we might prefer to have a better paid job and to go on luxurious holidays. In other words, if they could choose, many people would probably prefer the world to be more congenial in a material sense. Knowing that this is unlikely to be the case, there is a tendency for people to suffer.

Human beings also suffer because of the nature of their relationships with their fellow human beings. Parents watch their children gradually growing up and finally leaving home. They want their children to lead independent lives and yet at the same time they suffer through being parted from them. Such cycles of existence are almost inevitable and yet they still result in suffering. They have happened for countless generations and will continue to happen. The Buddha argued then that it is part of the human condition that people should live in a world that is unsatisfactory and which under normal circumstances will result in suffering. The next stage in the Buddha's reasoning was to try to go beyond the superficial causes of suffering, to analyse the fundamental reasons for suffering in human beings.

The Buddha's conclusion was that human suffering is not caused predominantly by the nature of the world, but by the reaction of human beings to it. This became the second Noble Truth. The Buddha argued that when people desire the world to be different from the way it is, particularly in those respects that are impossible to change, the result will be suffering. It is inevitable, for example, that one's body will get older and will not function as well. Whereas it might be sensible to take reasonable measures to slow down this process, such as eating healthy food and taking exercise, the final result cannot be changed. If therefore, one becomes attached too closely to the attempt to change this natural process, one will suffer. The acquiring of material possessions can also be a

> Buddhists acknowledge that the world is unsatisfactory, but
> see that the real problem of human existence is that we do
> not really understand how to relate to these circumstances.
> Once we understand the world as it really is, we can respond
> to it in a more effective manner.

cause of suffering. We might really want a new car. However,
when we get it, the novelty can wear off fairly quickly. The interior
soon gets a little dirty and the bodywork gets slight scratches.
Soon the excitement has gone and we again want something
new. Material possessions, argue Buddhists, are never ultimately
satisfying. They may please us for a very short time, but the
pleasure is soon replaced by unhappiness as we start to want
something else – perhaps something which it is unlikely we will
ever possess.

Therefore, just as the cause of suffering lies in the nature of
desires and the wish that things were different, the ceasing of
suffering can be achieved by the ending of desires. In other
words, if human beings could find a strategy to end the cycle
of having desires, then, according to Buddhists, their suffering
would largely cease. The possibility of ceasing suffering is the
third Noble Truth.

The Buddha did not stop here, however. He proposed a clear
strategy by which human beings could gradually reduce their
tendency to suffer. This strategy is the fourth Noble Truth,
otherwise known as the Noble Eightfold Path.

The first requirement of the Noble Eightfold Path is that the
Buddhist should hold 'Right Views'. One of the components
of this is that the individual should appreciate the nature of
impermanence. This should not be understood simply as a
theoretical concept, but rather as a phenomenon which can be seen
around us in the material world. The Buddhist should appreciate
that all phenomenal things eventually decay. There is nothing
which can prevent this and, moreover, the individual should

not become attached to anything in the material world, since attachment to the impermanent will ultimately lead to unhappiness.

The other component of 'Right Views' is the doctrine of 'no-self'. In a sense, this follows from the concept of impermanence. The individual human being is also impermanent and hence it can be argued that there is no permanent soul or self which can continue in existence after the death of the individual. If individuals can appreciate that there is no permanent self or identity then this probably helps in minimizing suffering, since there is no permanent entity to experience suffering.

The second feature of the Eightfold Path is usually described as 'Right Resolve'. By adhering to this the individual demonstrates a determination to be non-attached to the material world. This does require a determined decision since there is a tendency in many human beings to become attached to the superficially attractive and desirable. Right Resolve also involves the attitude of showing care and sensitivity towards our fellow human beings.

The next requirement on the Eightfold Path is Right Speech. This is a determination not to use speech in a manner which is unpleasant or to say harmful things either to or about another person. Buddhists are encouraged to be very mindful in the manner in which they speak. This means that they should never speak without careful thought, but should reflect before they speak.

Related to Right Speech is the requirement of Right Conduct. This prohibits the Buddhist from killing or harming living creatures in any way and also from immoral sexual conduct. Stealing is also prohibited under this aspect of the Eightfold Path. It should be noted that the regulations for monks and nuns are in many ways stricter than for non-ordained Buddhists. For example, monks and nuns are prohibited from any form of sexual activity.

The fifth component of the Eightfold Path is that the Buddhist should adopt a form of livelihood which does not involve, either directly or indirectly, the harming of other living things.

Occupations which have traditionally been prohibited include that of arms dealer and butcher or meat trader.

The three remaining components of the Eightfold Path are concerned with different aspects of meditation. 'Right Effort' is the term normally applied to the requirement for the Buddhist to be careful about making value judgements in relation to objects or people. In particular, Right Effort suggests that one should not allow thoughts of attraction or repulsion to develop in relation to anything. For example, if it is cold and raining one day, one is advised not to think that this is an awful and miserable day. To do so would be to make a value judgement about the nature of the day. One should simply think that it is raining and that the temperature is fairly low. Similarly, on a sunny day, one should not think that it is a wonderful, warm day. Rather, one should simply note that the sun is shining. For the Buddhist, the problem with allowing oneself to develop a sense of attraction to something is, first, that one becomes attached to the phenomenal world and second, that the individual tends to respond in a passive way to changes in stimuli from the world around.

'Right Attention' is the next element in the Eightfold Path. This encourages the person to be mindful of everyday events and functions. For example, the Buddhist, when walking, is encouraged to be mindful of the act of walking, to concentrate on the soles of the shoes touching the ground and of the feelings of the leg muscles. The same process of mindfulness should also be applied to functions such as sitting, standing, running, eating and breathing. One of the results of this technique is that it helps to prevent extraneous thoughts entering the mind, disturbing one's equanimity.

The final aspect of the Eightfold Path is 'Right Meditation'. A range of different techniques are used by Buddhists and two of these will be described shortly. Essentially, the purpose of the Eightfold Path and, in particular, of meditation is to enable the aspirant to see the true nature of the physical world and hence to avoid suffering. This condition of peace and tranquillity is known as *nirvana* or enlightenment.

Insight

Enlightenment is the ultimate aim of Buddhist practice. It is a condition in which we comprehend the real nature of existence, and hence can relate effectively to it. An enlightened person experiences peace and equilibrium, because they are able to relate calmly to the situations around them.

One common form of meditation employed in Buddhism is termed *anapanasati*, or meditation involving focusing attention on breathing. Essentially, the meditator sits in a cross-legged position and focuses attention on the inward and outward flowing of breath through the nostrils. There is nothing particular about the choice of breathing as the subject of meditation, except that it is a rhythmic, repetitive process that induces a sense of calm in the mind. Thus the prime purpose of *anapanasati* is to calm the mind and prepare it for the next stage of meditation.

Vipassana, or insight meditation, is the process whereby the meditator reflects on the thoughts which come and go in the mind. Even though one may have undergone a period of *anapanasati*, there may still be numerous thoughts which come and go. In *vipassana* meditation the purpose is to analyse these thoughts and learn from the process of reflection. The analysis is normally conducted according to three criteria. These are impermanence, suffering and no-self. (In Pali these terms are, respectively, *anicca*, *dukkha* and *anatta*.) Buddhists tend to employ these criteria in the following way. When a thought arises, they notice first of all that the thought is impermanent. No matter how significant, Buddhists argue that most thoughts tend to drift in to the mind and, given sufficient time, eventually drift out of the mind. Second, thoughts are frequently unsatisfactory. Even pleasant thoughts usually focus upon something which will not last for ever and hence if we attach to that thought, we will ultimately be disappointed. Finally, Buddhists feel that there is no permanent existing entity that 'owns' thoughts. There is no permanent 'self'. The thoughts are not 'mine'. They come and they go in a natural way. Thus, Buddhists employ these meditative techniques to try to understand the world in a clearer and more objective way. This description has tried to explain meditation as Buddhists employ the practice, but it should not be read as a guide to practical meditation. For the latter, Buddhists normally advise the beginner to obtain practical tuition from a reliable source.

The doctrinal division between Theravada, on the one hand, and Mahayana, on the other, reflected to some extent the role of laypeople in Buddhism. The Theravada tradition developed the reputation, rightly or wrongly, of focusing more on those who had been ordained. It was seen as a tradition through which monks and nuns could become enlightened. Although they could act as an inspiration for laypeople, there was perhaps a sense in which they occupied the central position in the tradition. The Mahayana tradition, however, arguably gave greater attention to the position of laypeople, particularly so with the concept of the *bodhisattva*. This was the notion of an enlightened person who delayed entering nirvana in order to be of assistance to others in helping them to gain enlightenment. Within the Mahayana also, there was something of a tendency for the Buddha himself to be regarded as an object of worship and veneration. This approach was antithetical to the Theravada tradition.

Ultimately, and by perhaps a strange irony, Buddhism virtually disappeared from India, its country of origin, being represented there mainly in the form of sacred sites visited by pilgrims. Nevertheless, Buddhism became firmly established in other countries, notably China, where the influential Ch'an school developed. This approach was very much devoted to the use of meditation techniques. The spread of Buddhism in China was much helped by the translation of Sanskrit Buddhist texts from India into Chinese. The *Lotus Sutra* was a particularly influential example, advocating as it did practices which were aimed at the salvation and enlightenment of all beings.

According to tradition, Ch'an Buddhism was taken to China at about the beginning of the sixth century CE by the Indian monk Bodhidharma. The word *ch'an* is the Chinese translation of the Sanskrit word *dhyana*, or meditation. As a school of Buddhism it sought to recapture the original experience of the Buddha during meditation. In a return to this direct experience of enlightenment, Ch'an did not accept some of the developments of ceremony and ritual which had taken place in Buddhism. One of the perhaps attractive features of Ch'an as a doctrine was that there was the potential for an immediate enlightenment experience, rather than one which had of necessity to be obtained through an extended period of meditation.

The Ch'an school of Buddhism also influenced the development of Buddhism in Japan, where it became known as *Zen*. The Japanese word 'zen' is cognate with the word 'ch'an' in Chinese. Like Ch'an Buddhism, Zen is centrally concerned with the meditation process. Eisai, a Japanese monk who had studied and meditated in China, is normally considered to have founded the Rinzai school of Zen. This uses the technique of the *koan* in order to help aspirants achieve enlightenment. The koan is a deliberately confusing and enigmatic saying which the monk or nun is asked to reflect upon and use as the object of meditation. A well-known example is: 'What is the sound of one hand clapping?' The alleged purpose of the koan is to prevent the mind engaging in too much rational, analytic thought which can prevent the attainment of enlightenment, or *satori*. Meditation which focuses upon the solution of the koan tends to involve more intuition than analytic thought and hence the possibility of a more rapid attainment of satori.

There also developed a separate school of Zen which was founded by a student of Eisai's called Dogen. He lived in the first part of the thirteenth century CE. This type of Buddhism was known as *Soto Zen*. In complete contrast to the Rinzai school, Soto Zen prescribed a gradualist approach to satori. In the Soto Zen monasteries there is an emphasis on ordinary everyday activities and the way in which a mindful approach to life can assist in gaining enlightenment. Soto Zen emphasizes the idea of non-attachment and this even applies to being non-attached to the idea of becoming enlightened!

Zen philosophy has had a great influence upon aesthetics in Japan,
particularly in areas such as painting, poetry, art, gardening
and calligraphy. There are some general Zen themes that are
identifiable in all these art forms. One of these is the concept of
emptiness, perhaps reflecting the emptiness of the enlightened
mind. In paintings, there are often large open spaces of sky or
water, with a solitary figure of, say, a monk, in one corner of
the painting. Equally, Zen gardens often consist of large open
spaces, such as expanses of neatly raked sand. A few boulders
may be carefully placed on the sand, and the whole abstract
composition employed as a subject for meditation. Quiet, natural
scenes are another common feature in Zen aesthetics. Again
such scenes are very common in Zen paintings, which may also
feature birds, animals, fruit or trees. Short Japanese poems
called *haiku* also commonly feature references to nature. Finally
perhaps one could argue that simplicity and minimalism are
features of Zen art. There is a general absence of decorative
effects, which is in some ways related to the use of the void,
mentioned earlier.

Organization

In a sense, anyone can be a Buddhist by following the Noble
Eightfold Path to the best of their abilities. It is not necessary to
be initiated in any way or to go through a form of entry rite. In
practical terms, however, if the person wishes to take the study
of Buddhism seriously, then it will probably be necessary to have
direct tuition from an experienced teacher and perhaps preferably
an ordained monk or nun. Buddhists may well argue that it is
desirable to attend a meditation class at a monastery.

Buddhist monasteries differ somewhat depending upon the particular 'school' of Buddhism and also through different cultural influences. Nevertheless, there are many general features in common and the following description provides a generalized account of a Theravada monastery. The central feature of the monastery is usually the meditation hall, in which the monks and nuns meditate and chant and in which laypeople can attend meditation sessions. Around the meditation hall will be located the individual huts of the monks and nuns. These may be distributed some distance apart. The huts will be very simple with only the most basic of amenities. Attached to the meditation hall, or nearby, there may be a kitchen and eating facilities.

The communal life of the monastery will start very early in the morning, say between 5 and 6 a.m. A monk will sound a bell to announce the imminent commencement of the morning meditation. The monks and/or nuns will sit in rows, with the head of the monastery near the image of the Buddha at one end of the meditation hall. The images of the Buddha which one tends to find in monasteries are not there as an object of worship or veneration, but simply as a reminder of the enlightenment experience of the Buddha and of the Buddha's teaching. It is this last aspect that is of real significance for Buddhists. The period of meditation usually starts with a period of chanting from the Pali scriptures, followed by a period of meditation lasting perhaps one hour. After this, the monks and nuns receive their first meal of the day, which will be something such as a bowl of gruel or porridge and a mug of tea. It is part of the Buddhist tradition that those who are ordained can only accept as food that which is given as alms by laypeople. They may not ask for the food, but only receive what is donated.

The morning may be devoted to work around the monastery. Each monk or nun may have allotted tasks ranging from gardening to looking after the library. Just before noon there is the main meal of the day. This will again consist of food which has been given as alms by laypeople. Those who have been ordained may not eat after noon each day. This is part of the Buddhist discipline which is concerned with simply eating sufficient to maintain the health of the body. The Buddhist would not wish to consume food purely for the 'delicious' taste or to satisfy the senses in any way. The emphasis is upon the functional use of food in maintaining the body.

In the afternoon, work around the monastery would again be undertaken and this might include some of the senior monks leading meditation classes for laypeople. In the early evening there will again be a period of chanting and meditation in the hall, on a similar basis to the early morning session. After the evening meditation, however, the head monk or nun may deliver a sermon or *dhamma* talk on a Buddhist theme. After sleep, the cycle of the day recommences.

The code of behaviour of *bhikkhus* (monks) is specified in terms of a range of precepts. Some of these are similar in content to the Eightfold Path, while others are more specifically related to the conduct of the lives of monks and nuns. They are forbidden from engaging in any kind of sexually oriented activity. There must be no consumption of alcohol or drugs for non-medicinal purposes. This is very much related to the notion of maintaining mindfulness. As these substances alter the response of the mind to the environment, it is impossible to consume them and remain mindful. Monks and nuns may not eat after midday. Again this is a means of using food simply as a functional necessity.

Ordained Buddhists do not watch or listen to music or entertainment. This is not to make a value judgement about these for laypeople, but rather to suggest that for *bhikkhus* they distract the mind and make the practice of mindfulness much more difficult, if not impossible. The structural organization of Buddhism within different countries depends to a large extent on the culture of each country. The history of Buddhism within Tibet offers a very interesting example of the integration and interaction of a religion with the secular administration of a country. Tibetan Buddhism is very much associated with the institution of the *Dalai Lama*. This title was established for the first time in the late fourteenth century and there gradually developed the notion of the reincarnation of the Dalai Lama. There is the assumption that each successive Dalai Lama is the reincarnation of the previous one. The present Dalai Lama is the 14th holder of the title and was born in 1935. He took up his role in 1940 as a young boy and subsequently had to flee Tibet for refuge in India, because of the unsuccessful challenge in 1959 to the rule of the Chinese. The title *dalai* means approximately 'ocean of wisdom' and the present Dalai Lama has become a noted world figure. In Tibet, prior to the rule of the Chinese, Buddhism was very much integrated with the non-religious organization of the country. Generally, however, one could argue that Buddhism has tended not to be as integrated with secular society as have some other major world religions which have been influential in, for example, a political sense.

10 THINGS TO REMEMBER

1 *Buddhism was founded by Siddhartha Gautama (approximately 563 BCE to 486 BCE).*

2 *His father was the ruler of a kingdom in what is now southern Nepal.*

3 *Siddhartha was brought up in relatively affluent circumstances.*

4 *One day, outside his father's palace, he reputedly encountered first an old man, then a sick man, then a corpse and finally a wandering ascetic.*

5 *This caused him to reflect upon the nature of existence.*

6 *He eventually left the palace and became a wandering ascetic.*

7 *Later, after a long period of meditation, he became spiritually enlightened and was known as the Buddha, or enlightened one.*

8 *He travelled to the Deer Park, just outside present-day Benares, and delivered his first sermon, expounding the basics of his philosophical system.*

9 *He ordained the first monks and founded the* sangha, *or community of Buddhists.*

10 *The* vinaya *is the code of conduct that governs the lifestyle of Buddhist monks and nuns.*

11

Jainism

In this chapter you will learn about:
- *the life of Mahavira*
- *the ascetic way of life in Jainism*
- *non-violence in Jainism.*

History

Jainism is one of the oldest religious traditions in India and is of approximately the same antiquity as Buddhism. The person normally regarded as the initiator of Jainism is the sage Vardhamana or, as he is normally known, Mahavira. The latter name may be translated as 'great hero' and the dates of Mahavira's life are approximately 599 to 527 BCE. He was born near the present-day city of Patna in the Indian state of Bihar. Relatively little in terms of detail is known of Mahavira's life, but it appears that he was the son of a relatively wealthy local ruler named Siddhartha, who belonged to the kshatriya caste. It may reasonably be assumed that he was brought up in fairly affluent surroundings and yet, at the age of about 30, he abandoned this security for the life of an itinerant *sadhu* or religious mendicant.

Such a lifestyle would entail abandoning possessions and money and having very limited contact with friends and family. Most of the life of a sadhu would be spent in meditation and yoga and wandering, perhaps in the company of other sadhus, from one holy place to another. It may seem strange that someone would relinquish a wealthy inheritance for such a life and yet this is not uncommon in present-day India. There are many sadhus in contemporary India and although they are not always regarded with respect by conventional society, there is a general feeling that the mendicant way of life is a valid lifestyle. It appears that Mahavira led this type of life for about ten or 11 years and then attained a form of enlightenment. After that he began to teach and to gather around him a number of disciples. As a fully enlightened being, he is known by Jains as a *jina*, or conqueror, i.e. one who has overcome the cycle of birth and rebirth. Mahavira is reputed to have ended his own life through voluntary starvation.

Although Mahavira is regarded as the founder of Jainism, a strict interpretation of Jain religious history sees Mahavira as the last in a long line of enlightened teachers. In common with Hindu notions of cosmology, Jains understand the universe as existing in a series of cycles, each of which has occupied an enormous expanse of time. Each cycle includes a period when the universe is expanding, and a corresponding period when the universe is contracting. During each cycle there appears a total of 24 enlightened spiritual teachers called *tirthankaras*. This word means 'fordmaker' and indicates that these sages have themselves crossed the stream of existence and escaped the eternal round of birth and death. Moreover, besides having achieved *moksha*, or release, themselves, they are also able through their teaching to assist others to gain enlightenment. Mahavira is seen by Jains as the last, the 24th, of the current series of tirthankaras, and hence to some extent it is inappropriate to view Jain history as starting with Mahavira. It should arguably start much earlier.

When Mahavira died, doctrinal divisions started to emerge within Jainism and this resulted in the development of at least two significant groupings. The *Svetambara* group, which means 'white robed', felt it was a sufficient mark of asceticism to wear simple white robes. In contrast, the *Digambaras* went naked. Members considered that for true ascetics it was necessary to relinquish the wearing of clothing. Digambaras also did not consider that women were capable of participating in the spiritual and organizational life of the monastic tradition. The Svetambaras, however, had a much more inclusive attitude to women members of the tradition.

Mahavira's teachings were originally transmitted orally. This was much the case with a number of other major religions. Eventually, however, it became necessary to produce his teachings in written form, in order to ensure their continuity and accuracy. A council was held at Valabhi in 456 CE and at this large conference the Svetambara teachings were enshrined in written form. During medieval times, a number of Jain monks who were also eminent scholars wrote analyses of the scriptures. Jain monks also became well known for their writings in the fields of literature and poetry.

The ultimate spiritual goal in Jainism is similar to that in Hinduism. In other words, the individual seeks to escape from the eternal cycle of life and death and hence attain *moksha*, or release. The principal method for attaining moksha is a life of asceticism. The other key feature of the Jain way of life is non-violence, or *ahimsa*, and in this respect Jainism and Jains exerted a significant influence on Mahatma Gandhi. During the period from about 900 CE to 1100 CE, the Jain community expanded considerably and Jain monks were responsible for a considerable amount of philosophical and spiritual writing. Jains were also the recipients of a good deal of royal patronage.

In modern India the Jain community probably exerts an influence out of all proportion to its total size of about three million people. Jains have become extremely successful in business, commerce and industry and are, relatively speaking, an affluent community. The main concentration of Jains in contemporary India is in the states of Gujarat, Maharashtra and Madhya Pradesh. In recent years Jains have increasingly emigrated from India and settled in the United States and England. In England, there are Jain communities in London and Leicester, where a very large and well-known Jain temple has been constructed.

Belief system

A central feature of Jain culture is that both monks and nuns and also, to a certain extent, laypeople, make a virtue of asceticism. The purpose of their respect for the ascetic way of life is partly to draw a distinction between the Jain way of life and a more materialistic existence. In addition, however, asceticism is seen as the primary means of helping to ensure that the individual can escape from the cycle of birth and death and hence attain salvation. An ascetic, spiritual lifestyle is thus perceived as the principal method of removing the effects of karma.

Insight

Asceticism is also very common in Hinduism, particularly among *sadhus*, and various types of renunciation are found in other religions too, where forms of abstinence are associated with religious devotion.

Jains perceive the universe as being very much determined by the law of cause and effect. In other words, from a philosophical point of view, each event in the universe has a cause and this operates on both a material and a spiritual level. If a person acts inappropriately, with anger or greed for example, then their soul will be affected and will accrue karma. The effect of this karmic accumulation is that the soul cannot escape from the consequence of rebirth. Jains believe that the process of karma involves the addition of a karmic substance to the soul. Such a substance is actually material in nature and becomes physically attached to the soul. The only way to eliminate the karma is for the individual to live a life of asceticism. This helps to loosen the karma and release the soul, which then has the potential to escape from the cycle of rebirth. The life of asceticism should include a number of other characteristics such as non-violence, meditation, vegetarianism and periodic fasting. Jains do not place a great deal of emphasis upon the concept of god, but perhaps emphasize more the total effect of those individuals whose souls have escaped the cycle of birth and death.

Non-violence, or *ahimsa*, remains a very significant feature of Jain life. Some groups of monks go to great lengths to try to ensure that they do not harm any living things. Some carry a small brush or broom with which to sweep the path as they are walking along. They hope in this way to gently clear the path of small insects that they might otherwise tread on and kill. Equally, some groups wear a small gauze or linen face mask, which, it is hoped, excludes small insects that might fly into the mouth and be killed or consumed. These strategies indicate the importance that Jains attach to the principle of non-violence. The same principle is continued in the attitudes and way of life of Jains where it is considered unacceptable for example to behave in an aggressive manner or to try to acquire additional material possessions in a greedy manner. The concept of ahimsa is seen as a very important ethical principle that should be an integral part of the daily life of Jains. Moreover, Jains are not expected to have an occupation that involves harming other human beings or animals in any way. It is for this reason that Jains rarely take part in agriculture or become farmers, since the digging of the soil almost inevitably involves killing small soil organisms. Hence many Jains have opted for occupations within financial services or business where there is no overt sense of aggression.

Insight

A philosophy of non-violence is found in many religions. It is related to the idea of respecting fellow human beings and not acting in a way that might harm them.

Organization

The organization of the Jain religion is predicated upon the idea of following the basic teachings of Mahavira, i.e. an ascetic life-style which incorporates the notion of ahimsa, or non-violence. In their turn, these principles of life are aimed at the individual being able to shed the accumulation of karma and escape the endless cycle of birth and rebirth. It is assumed, however, that laypeople are unable, for a variety of reasons, to lead a sufficiently ascetic life to achieve the goal of salvation. It is not seen as being a lack of religious motivation on the part of laypeople that prevents their achieving this goal, but rather that they typically have a large number of commitments to family and friends which make it impossible for them to adopt the ascetic life with the required single-mindedness. There is, however, a prescribed pattern of conduct for laypeople, which involves considerable renunciation, and which enables them to eliminate some karmic effects. Such a discipline may have the benefit of enabling the individual to be born into a situation where s/he can live the ascetic life of a monk or nun and hence obtain salvation within the duration of that life.

It is thus necessary for a person who aspires to achieve salvation to become ordained and to live the monastic, ascetic life. The ascetic dimension of the monk's life is sometimes considerable and novice monks, for example, traditionally have the hairs pulled out of their head one by one at ordination, rather than having their head shaved. The novice commits to five basic principles of life, which have parallels in the lives of many Hindu and Buddhist monastic orders. They commit to not owning anything, since possessions may become a responsibility and hence divert the person from the religious life. There is a very definite commitment to the principles of non-violence, which involves not causing physical harm to other living creatures and also not speaking unkindly and not behaving inconsiderately.

Insight

Non-violence includes refraining from speaking in a thoughtless, and hence unkind manner. In other words, besides the act of refraining from physical damage to anyone, there is also an attempt to be mindful in terms of the way in which one speaks to people.

Jain monks will typically filter the water they drink in order to avoid swallowing and killing small organisms in the water. In addition, the novice is expected to refrain from stealing, from sexual activity and from lying. Novices are also usually given an alms bowl in which to collect food alms. The practice of collecting food alms helps to establish a positive and spiritual relationship between monks and nuns and the lay community. Laypeople have the opportunity to accumulate good karmic consequences by helping to support the mendicant community. It is a positive action that can help to build up karmic merit. For monks too there are a number of positive spiritual effects that derive from their dependence upon food alms. First of all, in the process of depending on alms food, they cannot choose foods which are particularly tasty or appealing. Essentially, they have only what they are given. This helps to develop an attitude of mind which is very detached from the material world. There is little purpose in desiring certain kinds of food, because these simply may never be given as alms. Hence one has to be happy and thankful for what is given as alms. If it is too much, too little or not cooked just as one likes it, all these factors become of little consequence. In addition, the monk or nun cannot predict whether they will be given any food at all and hence the dependence on food alms further emphasizes the need to be detached from the material world.

Insight

The act of living on alms encourages Jain monks and nuns to place themselves in the hands of their fellow human beings. This tends to emphasize the sense of interrelationship between people.

Mendicants will typically spend much of the year wandering in small groups to pilgrimage places. The exception is in the rainy season when travel becomes difficult and they usually return to the monastery of their original teacher or guru. During this time they study, meditate and provide spiritual guidance and instruction for the laypeople of the surrounding area who visit the monastery.

The monks and nuns have a number of characteristic features associated with monastic practice. One of these is to cultivate a mental state of peace and harmony, which results in feelings of complete integration with one's surroundings. The mental condition as described tends to be developed through the process of meditation, which is a regular feature of Jain religious practice. The purpose of the meditation practice is to make the monk or nun completely aware of their surroundings, so that their minds do not wander to irrelevant thoughts. Hence they live very much in the present, being totally aware of their bodies and their surroundings. Although thoughts do come and go in their minds, they learn not to become preoccupied with them. The attainment of such a state of equanimity is one of the principal goals of the mendicants. In addition, monks and nuns also regularly ask forgiveness for not keeping any of the principal requirements of the monastic lifestyle. Such transgressions may only be extremely insignificant, yet are still important to the monks and nuns because of the sensitive nature of their lifestyle.

The goal of the Jains' monastic lifestyle can be summed up by saying that it is an attempt to detach themselves from the materialist nature of everyday life. In so doing they gain from the spiritual dimension of life. Perhaps the ultimate manifestation of detachment from the material world is the act of the Jain mendicant fasting to death in later life. This act of voluntarily relinquishing life is seen as an example of not being attached to the pleasures of the phenomenal world. It is also regarded as being a non-violent death. It is regarded by Jains as being an ideal way of departing this world.

Laypeople emulate the lifestyle of monks and nuns to some considerable extent. They aspire to the same ideals as mendicants but cannot, because of everyday obligations, fulfil all of these to the extent required to obtain release from the eternal cycle of reincarnation. They, too, ask for forgiveness for transgressions from the Jain ideals of life. The Jain concept of the universe does not involve the idea of a single deity who has created the universe. There is not therefore the notion of the act of worship of a deity within the Jain temple. However, it is the practice to worship statues of the tirthankaras as embodiments of the Jain ideal of life. It is common practice for both mendicants and laypeople to conduct acts of puja or worship before these statues. Flowers will be brought to the temple and incense lit.

The Jain religion involves a very sensitive interpretation of the world around us. It is based on an ideal of not impacting upon and hence damaging any aspect of our surroundings – thus evolved the ideal of non-violence. The material world is seen as fundamentally unsatisfactory and leading ultimately to unhappiness. Therefore the Jain seeks to eliminate attachment to the material world and the key way to accomplish this is through the ascetic approach to life.

Insight

The ideal of living in harmony with one's surroundings is also found in Hinduism and Buddhism. It is in Jainism, however, that the ideal of a non-violent life has been so extensively developed, and integrated throughout the religion.

10 THINGS TO REMEMBER

1 *The founder of Jainism was Mahavira.*

2 *He was born near Patna in India and lived from approximately 599* BCE *to 527* BCE.

3 *At about the age of 30 he became a* sadhu, *or wandering religious mendicant.*

4 *He is known by Jains as a* jina, *or conqueror – that is, someone who has overcome the cycle of birth and rebirth.*

5 *Mahavira is thought to have ended his life through voluntary starvation.*

6 *On Mahavira's death, there developed two main doctrinal divisions among Jains.*

7 *The Digambaras felt that, as ascetics, they should not wear any clothes.*

8 *The Svetambaras, however, wore simple white robes.*

9 *The spiritual goal of Jains is* moksha, *or release from the cycle of birth and rebirth.*

10 *Jains place great emphasis upon asceticism.*

12

....

The religion of the Parsis

In this chapter you will learn about:
- *the origins of Zoroastrianism*
- *religious customs of the Parsis*
- *ethics of the Parsi way of life*.

_____

History

The religion of the Parsis is a form of Zoroastrianism, which was
the original religion of Iran, before the arrival of Islam. Some
Zoroastrians migrated to India, settled in the region of Bombay
and gradually adapted to some extent to the indigenous Hindu
culture.

Zoroastrianism was founded by Zoroaster, or Zarathustra, who
was born in Iran and lived in approximately 1500 BCE. Much of
Zoroaster's teaching may have had some indirect influence upon
the development of Judaism and hence Christianity.

Zoroaster appears to have experienced a series of visions of God,
and to have evolved a theology based upon two quite different
divinities. For Zoroaster, the noblest divinity, and the one which
represented all the qualities of goodness in the universe, was Ahura
Mazda. Posed in opposition to Ahura Mazda, however, was a
divinity which represented the negative and evil influences of the

universe. One could argue that this concept is a form of metaphor, which mirrors the choices that human beings must make between goodness and wickedness. The Zoroastrian scriptural texts are known as the *Avesta* and contain, among other writings, the *Gathas* or early hymns.

Significant parts of the *Avesta* are written in a language called Avestan. Later Zoroastrian scriptural texts were written in Persian. Within the Zoroastrian tradition there was a strong tendency to emphasize life after death and the notion that God would reward those who had behaved ethically during life. Zoroaster abandoned many traditional sacrifices and to this extent he was a religious reformer. He did, however, retain within his system the fire ceremonies, which are often associated with Zoroastrianism.

When Muslim influence spread into Persia, Zoroastrianism was gradually replaced as the dominant religion. It did, however, remain intact in several localized regions, within a sect called the Gabars. At first there was no great conflict between the Muslims and the Zoroastrians, but eventually, by approximately the eighth century CE, relationships between the two religions deteriorated and groups of Zoroastrians began to emigrate. At first they settled at Hormuz on the Persian Gulf, but later migrated to the state of Gujarat in India. There they were accepted by the indigenous Hindus and became a well-integrated agricultural community, looking after their cattle and raising crops.

The indigenous people knew them as 'Parsis', or Persians, an indication of their country of origin. The Parsis lived a fairly unchanging life for a number of centuries until, in about the seventeenth century, there was a considerable expansion of trade and industry in the Gujarat area. The Parsi community appeared to be able to adapt readily to business and commerce and became increasingly wealthy. The acquisition of Bombay by the East India Company in 1668 was a further factor in the industrial and commercial expansion of the region. After this, many Parsis moved to the growing city of Bombay.

It is generally true that the Parsi community and the British in India felt a certain cultural affinity. Although Zoroastrianism and Christianity were very different religions, there was a sense in which they both seemed to have similar value systems. As Bombay developed as a centre for commercial and industrial activities, the British administration made it economically advantageous for people to move to the Bombay area and this was a further encouragement to the commercial enhancement of the region. Within this environment, the Parsi community flourished and became very successful economically.

A love of education for its own sake had for many years been a significant feature of Zoroastrian culture. Not only was this respect for education shared by the British, but also the Parsis had considerable affinity with the content and style of British education. The Parsi attraction to British education had the effect of helping them to acquire some of the cultural characteristics of a people they admired. In addition it enabled Parsis to enter the most prestigious occupations and professions and indeed to exercise an influence in the Bombay area quite out of proportion to their actual numbers in the population. To further their devotion to education, the Parsi community built schools. Commercial success brought other results as well, including considerable success and influence in Indian politics, at both a local and national level.

In the late fifteenth century, the Parsis attempted to renew the relationship with their ancestral group in Persia. However, perhaps through the effects of time and separation, it was evident that there were by now some cultural and doctrinal differences.

As the Parsi community became wealthier during the period of British colonialism, small groups of Parsis emigrated and established communities in different parts of the world. A Parsi community became established in Kenya, for example, towards the end of the nineteenth century and accumulated considerable wealth through trade and commerce. There were other communities in Australia and the United States. The small group of Parsis who settled in England were also successful and, as one indicator, two Parsis became members of parliament in the late 1800s.

Belief system

Zoroaster believed that the world in which human beings had been born was characterized by the conflict between goodness and evil. Human beings had definite moral choices to make in this world and it behoved them to lead a good and noble way of life. God was known as Ahura Mazda, or simply Mazda, and was seen as possessing all the noble and virtuous characteristics of existence. According to Zoroaster, human beings should choose to live a life of goodness rather than evil and to follow the spiritual inspiration of Mazda. God was considered to have created human beings and in particular the facets of mankind which are, on the one hand, material and, on the other, spiritual. Mazda also gave mankind the capacity for free will and with it the ability to opt for a noble and spiritual life, on the one hand, or to be ensnared by an evil existence, on the other. Zoroaster was also very keen to specify the noble qualities to which human beings should aspire and which they should attempt to have in common with Mazda. These noble, virtuous qualities included such notions as righteousness, devotion and the cultivation of a 'good' mind. Zoroaster was of the firm belief that, in the final analysis, there would be a triumph of the noble and virtuous over evil. Zoroaster placed a great emphasis on living an ethical life and avoiding acts of violence.

The *Avesta* are the scriptures which are thought by Zoroastrians to contain spiritual messages sent from God to humanity via the medium of the prophet Zoroaster. Followers of Zoroaster believe that the poems and hymns of the Avesta, because they are the word of God, contain absolute truth. For Zoroastrians, fire is the eternal symbol of truth from God. In the Zoroastrian fire temples, the priests who maintain the fires wear shields over the lower part of their face, as they believe this helps sustain the purity of the flames. Fire is a metaphor for the spirit of life within human beings. The sacred fires in the fire temples are supposed to be always maintained and the priests place fuel on them five times or more each day.

The essence of the Zoroastrian spiritual life can be summed up in a variety of principles for ethical living. Zoroaster regarded human beings as being characterized by the phenomenon of reason and hence having the capacity to select between good and evil. Having the capacity to make moral choices also gives people a sense of human will. In other words, the human being is able to chart a moral course through life and hence have a sense of spiritual direction.

Insight

The emphasis upon reason and rational moral decision-making encourages the idea of active participation in the world, as opposed to the notion of ascetic withdrawal from the world, which is found in some other faiths.

Education is regarded as very important for Zoroastrians, since the person devoted to education is seen as being capable of developing wisdom and, as a consequence of this, a sense of moral probity and balance. The spiritual person is expected to sustain a type of lifestyle which creates a sense of equilibrium between the needs of the physical body and the needs of the spirit. Human beings should look after their health and should do so by trying to avoid extremes in all things.

Insight

The emphasis on education encourages the Parsi community to learn about other faiths, and combined with a respect for rational thought, this encourages a spirit of tolerance towards other religions.

Perhaps one factor in the success of the Parsi community has been their willingness to adapt to the host Hindu and Muslim communities in the Indian subcontinent. Thus they have generally avoided eating pork and beef and many have become vegetarian. Such policies have prevented their coming into direct conflict with Muslims and Hindus respectively. Within Zoroastrianism there have traditionally been seven holy days during the year, the most important of these being the day devoted to the worship of fire, which represents the notion of goodness overcoming evil.

There is a general acceptance within the Parsi faith that light is representative of what is good and noble in the world, while darkness represents that which is unethical. As a result of this belief system, Parsis are often reluctant to carry out a number of activities during darkness, simply because it is regarded as inauspicious. In a somewhat related sense, fire is not put out deliberately, as this would imply the willing transition from lightness to darkness. Rather, flames are left to expire gradually by themselves.

Parsis normally pray when the sun is rising, at midday, in the evening, at midnight and then at dawn. Prayers would ideally be said in front of the sacred fire, as symbolic of moral behaviour. To accompany the prayers, verses from the *Gathas* are also often recited. Cleanliness is very important to Parsis and, before prayers are said, a Parsi will normally engage in ritual washing.

Organization

For the Parsis, fire is extremely sacred because of its assumed purity. Temples where the sacred flame is maintained are the focus of religious activity. Such fire temples are known in Gujarati as *agiari*. Sometimes it is felt necessary to establish a new holy fire and this process is accompanied by a long ceremony. Temples are not uniform in design and architecture, but generally have at least some common features. There is the prayer room used largely for private prayers and which contains the sacred fire. In another room the priest conducts religious ceremonies, usually in the absence of laypeople, although people who have not been ordained may witness such ceremonies. Finally, there is a large room which is used by laypeople for events such as weddings. The devotee may attend the temple at any reasonable time which is convenient.

Upon entering the temple, the devotee usually performs standard ablutions and recites certain prayers. These practices are designed to create feelings of calm and spirituality, before the devotee enters the temple proper. The devotee then pauses to look at a picture of Zoroaster, which is designed to engender a feeling of spirituality. Then the devotee moves to the prayer room, removes footwear and covers the head. After prayers, pieces of sandalwood are left for the priest to put on the flames later.

The sacred flames of the fire temples have several different symbolic meanings for Parsis. As the flames flicker upwards while burning, there is a reminder for Parsis that they should lift up their thoughts to God. Parsis feel that the fire is the same for all of humanity and hence it is a reminder of the equality of all people. As sandalwood is often burned, the scent reminds devotees of the beauty of the life of the spirit.

One of the characteristic features of the Parsi religious life is the method used for the disposal of the dead. In the original culture of Iran, it was almost certainly the custom to leave dead bodies untended, where they would be rapidly consumed by wolves, jackals or other scavenging animals. This original practice has evolved in the Indian context into a ritualized disposal of the dead in so-called Towers of Silence. These are specially created buildings in which the dead are exposed to the sky and are consumed by vultures.

Parsis see this method as having a number of practical advantages. The bodies are consumed very rapidly and, in a warm climate, this minimizes the spread of disease. It is perhaps a slightly more philosophical point, but it is seen as a rapid and efficient means of recycling organic matter in the environment. In a more religious sense, Parsis see cremation and burial as being more polluting methods of disposal and see the Towers of Silence as being a cleaner method. The remaining bones are dried by the sun and then pushed into a central pit.

Parsis believe that, after death, they are judged by God in terms of the moral and religious nature of the lives they have led. They conceive of a bridge across which one may walk to the heaven occupied by Ahura Mazda. To either side of the bridge, however, there is a precipitous drop to hell. Only those who have led the religious life manage to walk across the bridge and thus reach heaven. Parsis view human life as a continuous struggle against the ritual contamination which accompanies death. Hence, they attempt to celebrate the existence of light and life.

10 THINGS TO REMEMBER

1 *The Parsi religion is derived from Zoroastrianism, the original religion of Iran.*

2 *Zoroastrianism was founded by Zoroaster (or Zarathustra), who lived from approximately 630 BCE to 550 BCE.*

3 *Zoroaster was a monotheist who worshipped a single deity, Ahura Mazda.*

4 *The Zoroastrian scriptures are known as the Avesta.*

5 *Zoroaster believed that there were moral choices to be made in the world and that people should act ethically and virtuously.*

6 *Ahura Mazda had given human beings a free will and Zoroaster wanted people to exercise that free will to act morally.*

7 *In the eighth century CE, a group of Zoroastrians emigrated from Persia to the state of Gujarat in India.*

8 *The people of Gujarat knew them as 'Parsis', or Persians.*

9 *When Bombay expanded in the eighteenth and nineteenth centuries, many Parsis moved there and became involved in business and commerce.*

10 *Parsis have temples in which a sacred flame is maintained, as a symbol of the truth of God.*

13

Sikhism

In this chapter you will learn about:
* *the lives and teachings of the Sikh Gurus*
* *the religious philosophy of the Sikh scripture, the Guru Granth Sahib*
* *the role of the gurdwara in Sikh religious practice.*

History

The Sikh religion was founded in Panjab in India by Guru Nanak, who was born in 1469 at Talwandi. His father was a village administrator. As a child, Nanak was reputedly very able at school, mastering Persian and Arabic, among other languages. Although he was born a Hindu, Nanak was from an early age fairly critical of some of the traditional practices of his family faith. As an adolescent he is reported to have been impractical by nature and to have enjoyed solitary reflection and contemplation.

At the age of about 16 he was married to a girl called Sulakhni, and they subsequently had two sons, called Sri Chand and Lakhmi Das. Nanak did not adjust readily to the responsibilities of being a family man and retained a longing for the spiritual life. He did not settle easily into stable employment and, as a result of this, his sister, Nanaki, and her husband, Jai Ram, invited Nanak to Sultanpur, where they asked their employer to give Nanak a job.

This their employer did and Nanak was placed in charge of the local store and in particular of keeping the accounts. Although Nanak created a very good impression in this post, he eventually became dissatisfied with the work, leaving the job and joining a group of *sadhus* or itinerant religious ascetics.

Later, Nanak embarked on a series of very long pilgrimages to cities which were holy to both Hindus and Muslims. He was accompanied by a family servant called Mardana. Mardana was a Muslim and had been a very close friend of Nanak for a long time. Nanak travelled eastwards as far as Benares, to Sri Lanka in the south and the Himalayas in the north. He also travelled as far as Mecca in the west. He visited the holy places of other religions, partly to study them but also to be able to comment on features of the practice of these faiths. As a general theme, Nanak tended to be critical of religious rites and ceremonies which were treated as very important and yet had no real basis to be considered in this way.

Eventually, after many years of travelling, Nanak settled in Kartarpur and took up the life of a peasant farmer, while at the same time remaining heavily involved in his religious duties. He built a *dharamsala*, or set of buildings which housed members of the emerging Sikh community. At this dharamsala he introduced the custom of the *langar*, or communal meal, which was open to all castes and which was free from the rituals normally associated with Hinduism. Guru Nanak always practised and advocated principles which could be described as egalitarian. For example, he spoke in Panjabi, which was the language of ordinary people in that part of northern India, rather than employing Sanskrit, as used traditionally by the brahmin priests. Guru Nanak died in 1539 CE and shortly before his death he named one of his disciples, Lehna, to succeed him as the leader of the Sikh community. Lehna subsequently became known as Guru Angad. All the subsequent Sikh Gurus followed the same practice of nominating their successors as leaders of the community.

Guru Angad (1504–52) made an extremely significant contribution to the developing Sikh tradition by developing the *Gurmukhi* script for writing the words of Guru Nanak and also for secular communication in Panjabi. Gurmukhi has the capacity to represent all vowel sounds and hence it can be used to transcribe the spoken word with accuracy. It also enabled the Sikh scriptural writings to have a distinctive character of their own, which made a contribution to the establishment of a distinctive Sikh culture. In the past Sanskrit had always been associated with the brahminical caste and hence with arguably an elitist approach to religion. The development of Gurmukhi was one factor in the democratization of religious practice among the Sikhs, since it enabled the scriptures to be transcribed in the language of the majority of the community.

As a further example of the democratic nature of Sikh society, Guru Angad emphasized the function of the langar and its usefulness in breaking down social barriers based on social class and caste. In addition, the Guru reflected the importance of practical work to support the religious and spiritual life, by earning his living through weaving grass ropes.

Guru Angad's emphasis on the role of the langar was further stressed by the next Guru, Amar Das (1479–1574). Guru Amar Das became the Guru in 1552 and instituted a system whereby anyone of whatever importance who came to meet him had first to eat a meal at the langar. He even applied this regulation to Akbar, the Emperor of India. From the days of its early development, Sikhism had always argued that the spiritual life should be combined with the everyday life of earning a living. Guru Amar Das argued successfully that religious ascetics could not be accepted within the Sikh community because they typically depended on alms for food, rather than earning their own living to support themselves.

Guru Ram Das, who succeeded Guru Amar Das, lived from 1534 to 1581 CE. He was well known as the founder of Amritsar, the town in Panjab which is the location for the Golden Temple, the spiritual centre of the Sikh religion. Under Guru Ram Das, business enterprises were encouraged to become established at Amritsar and hence the town grew in size and importance. It was

of considerable importance for the Sikh community to have a place
of pilgrimage and devotion specifically associated with their religion.

Guru Arjan (1563–1606) was the next Sikh Guru and he was well
known for starting the building of the temple at Amritsar which
would become known as the Golden Temple. The foundation stone
of the temple was laid by a Muslim saint named Mian Mir. This
was perhaps a significant demonstration of the religious tolerance
of the Sikhs. Another demonstration of such tolerance is that the
temple was constructed with an entrance on each of the four sides,
thus demonstrating an openness to all ideas, faiths and castes
of people. Guru Arjan tried to encourage Sikhs to become good
horseriders and to keep horses. Such prowess was later to become
important as the Sikh community developed a military awareness.

Guru Arjan was also of great importance because of his role in
compiling the *Adi Granth*, the Sikh scripture. Besides the hymns of
the Sikh Gurus, he also included in the *Adi Granth* the writings of
Hindu and Muslim saints, again an illustration of respect for other
religions. The holy book was prepared and placed in the Golden
Temple in 1604. There was a sense in which the Sikh community
gradually became politicized during the leadership of Guru Arjan
and it is possible that he supported an opponent of the Emperor
Jehangir. The result was that the Emperor ordered the Guru's
arrest and later execution at Lahore.

Guru Hargobind (1595–1644) was the son of Guru Arjan and
was notable for taking his father's advice about establishing a
Sikh army. Guru Hargobind urged his fellow Sikhs to keep a
sword and to amass a collection of horses. The end result was
that it was possible to sustain an army to protect the growing
Sikh community. Guru Hargobind was also responsible for the
establishment of the *Akal Takht*, a building next to the Golden
Temple, which became the focus for the secular and administrative
activities of Sikhs.

Har Rai was the Sikh Guru from 1630 to 1661. The Emperor
Aurangzeb asked to see Guru Har Rai, but the latter sent his son

Ram Rai for the audience with the Emperor. During the audience Ram Rai reputedly recited some verses from the *Adi Granth*, but made an error during the recitation. Some thought that this was due to nervousness in front of the Emperor. When the Guru heard of this he was extremely annoyed as he felt it essential that the Sikhs always displayed courage. There was a sense in which the Sikh community was embattled at all times and the demonstration of personal courage became, so it was felt, a necessary requirement for the continuity and survival of Sikhs.

The next Guru, Har Krishan (1656–64), died before he was able to fulfil his potential for the Sikhs. The ninth Guru was Tegh Bahadur, who lived from 1621 to 1675. He developed a reputation as a soldier who had fought against the Muslim rulers of India. The Guru encouraged the maintenance of a Sikh army and the Emperor of India, Aurangzeb, became increasingly disenchanted with his political activities. In particular the Guru offered protection and support to Hindus whom Aurangzeb had attempted to convert forcibly to Islam. Tegh Bahadur was eventually arrested and taken to Delhi with a group of other Sikhs, where the Guru and two of his friends were executed.

The son of Tegh Bahadur, Gobind Singh, became the next Sikh Guru. He lived from 1666 to 1708. Gobind Singh was nine years old when his father was executed. A faithful friend of Tegh Bahadur brought the executed Guru's severed head to show to Gobind Singh. In 1676 Gobind Singh was officially made the tenth Sikh Guru.

One of his first acts was to establish an armed town to which he encouraged many Sikhs to move. This town was known as Paunta. The Sikhs undertook regular military training, combined with the saying of the accepted prayers. In 1687 Guru Gobind Singh's first child was born. In 1706 the Guru added the hymns of his father, Tegh Bahadur, to the *Adi Granth*. He also determined that from that point onwards there would not be another person as a Sikh Guru, but rather that the holy book of the Sikhs would become the Guru. Thus the scripture became known as the *Guru Granth Sahib*.

Guru Gobind Singh did not add any of his own hymns to the *Adi Granth*. These were placed in a separate volume, the *Dasam Granth*.

Guru Gobind Singh was also responsible for the foundation of the *Khalsa*, or community of initiated Sikhs. In 1699 he invited the Sikh community to gather at Anandpur and asked the gathered people how many of them would be prepared to lay down their lives for him. In some ways this may seem to have been a strange action, but it appears that there were some challenges to the authority of the Guru and he wished to inspire the Sikhs with his leadership, and also to generate a sense of his own personal authority. After a pause, one man came forward and the Guru took him into an adjoining tent. A few moments later the Guru emerged with his sword stained red. The people gathered there appeared to assume that it was blood and that the man had been sacrificed. The Guru then asked for more volunteers and, in turn, four more men came forward. The same thing happened each time. Then to the probable surprise and relief of the crowd, the five men appeared completely unharmed. Guru Gobind Singh announced that they were true examples of the bravery of Sikhs, and that from then onwards they would be known as the *Panj Pyare*, or the Five Beloved Ones.

The Guru then created the ceremony which is used to initiate people into the Sikh community. He took a metal bowl and poured water into it. The wife of the Guru then added sugar crystals to the water and the Guru dissolved them by stirring with a double-edged sword. The Panj Pyare then sipped the *amrit* or sugar solution and were thus regarded as being members of the Khalsa or community of initiated Sikhs. The Guru then asked the five new Khalsa members to initiate his wife and himself. This act was symbolic of the equality of all Khalsa members. Finally, the Guru invited all the people present to become initiated as members of the Khalsa. Many did so, but some refrained, apparently still concerned about the caste restrictions which they would have to discard.

From then on, Khalsa members adopted certain characteristics of physical appearance and dress, which to this day can be used to recognize Sikhs. There are five principal features, known as the five Ks, because the word for each in Panjabi begins with the letter K. In summary these features are that the Khalsa Sikh must not cut the hair; must wear a comb to maintain the hair in a tidy condition; should wear a steel bangle on the right wrist; should wear a sword; and finally wear a pair of shorts as underclothes.

After the death of Gobind Singh, there was no longer a person as the Sikh Guru. There followed a lengthy period of conflict with the Muslim rulers of India. Some Sikh leaders emerged who were not only political leaders but also warriors. Banda Singh became famous through his battles with the Muslims, but he was captured and executed by the Muslims in 1716 CE. There was some success at establishing a Sikh region of control and Ranjit Singh ruled a considerable area from his base in Lahore which he set up in 1799. In more recent times, there has been substantial pressure among parts of the Sikh community for the establishment of an independent Sikh country or state, provisionally named Khalistan. Some Sikhs, however, doubt whether the creation of such a state is ever likely to come to pass.

Partly as a result of the varied roles played by Sikhs during British rule in India, there has been considerable migration of Sikhs to different parts of the world in recent years. There are substantial Sikh communities in North America, for example, and in England Sikhs have settled in the London area, in the Midlands and in West Yorkshire. They tended to migrate initially to locations where there was the possibility of employment and, once there, became active in the community and usually established gurdwaras.

Belief system

In a strictly theological sense, the ultimate purpose of Sikhism can be argued to be a state of mystical union with God. It is this goal towards which spiritually minded Sikhs aspire. The term 'guru' has several different uses in Sikhism, but perhaps the most fundamental use is God as Guru who is revealed at least partly through the scripture of the *Adi Granth* or *Guru Granth Sahib*. God is also revealed, however, in the souls of people as the Word of God, or *sabad*. This is the manner in which God is present internally in people. In addition, God is present externally in the entire universe as a form of spiritual or moral order which guides the whole scheme of things. This moral energy which permeates the universe is termed the *hukam*. However, the Sikh would assert that the sabad and the hukam are not necessarily available to be seen by everyone, but that God's grace must be given to individuals before they can perceive the sabad and hukam. The basic concept of grace, or *nadar*, is that it does not of itself enable salvation to take place, but that it provides the individual with the ability to recognize the Word of God and hence to lead the type of life which will result in salvation. The hukam is seen as being a form of energy which enables the universe to function in an essentially ethical manner. God is able to transmit to people an awareness of the manner in which they can attain salvation. This is achieved through the means of the Word. Sikhs also use, to a certain extent, the original Hindu concept of karma. Karma, or the accumulated consequences of past actions, is related to the notion of grace. A karma derived from good actions is seen as having a positive effect on the transmission of God's grace. A good karma helps the individual to receive God's grace. Equally, if one tries seriously to live one's life in accordance with the hukam, then it is seen as being possible slowly to rectify the effects of adverse karma. Although God as Guru is seen as permeating the *Adi Granth*, which is available to be heard by all Sikhs, individuals still need to work hard to live a moral life, in order to work towards salvation. If one tries sincerely to live one's life in empathy with the hukam, or ethical order, then personal egoism, or *haumai*, will tend to be minimized.

One of the functions of the *Adi Granth* is to act as a medium of communication through which the hukam is transmitted from God to human beings. The *Adi Granth* is frequently used to provide advice for devout Sikhs on day-to-day problems and issues. It is not uncommon for Sikhs to open the *Adi Granth* at random early in the morning and to use the verses that appear on the selected page as inspiration for the day's activities. In order to attain salvation, one of the main requirements is for the Sikh to be able to demonstrate loving devotion towards the divine. There appears to be a relationship here with the Hindu bhakti tradition of devotion to a personal divinity and this may well be because Guru Nanak was himself brought up in a religious environment conditioned by this particular approach to God. A significant difference from the Hindu tradition, however, was that Guru Nanak did not accept the notion of a human form for God, as in the case of some of the statues in Hindu temples.

For Sikhs the sum total of God's qualities are encapsulated in the name, or *nam*, of God. Within each human being there exists the presence of the divine Guru and salvation may only be attained by the individual person recognizing this presence and acting in accordance with the hukam.

Another significant difference between the Hindu and Sikh traditions is that Guru Nanak had no liking for religious ritual. He felt that to express devotion to objects was often a misplaced devotion, because objects often lost their original spiritual significance. More important for salvation was to discover the presence of the Guru in everyday life and within oneself. In addition to this, the individual should express devotion to God's Word, or sabad, and to God's name, or nam.

Insight

Worship in the gurdwara tends to be focused upon the words of the *Guru Granth Sahib*, and the teachings of the different Gurus. There are not the complex ceremonies which are found in some religions.

Sikhism has never truly been a proselytizing faith. Although it has gladly received converts, there has not been a plan to attract people from other religions. Indeed, the general approach has been to encourage people to follow the basic tenets of their own faith and to express their religious faith within that context. Besides this strong sense of tolerance for other faiths, Sikhs have always had a strong social sense. They feel that helping society is an expression of the divine hukam and one of the necessary conditions for salvation. It is felt that all one's deeds should be devoted to God.

One of the greatest obstacles to salvation, however, is that of *haumai*, or self-centredness. Haumai may also be translated as egoism or self-interest. Haumai is the act of doing something for one's own benefit rather than devoting that action to God. Sikhs believe that while people are attached to egoism, this can only result in the continued transmigration of the soul. The main strategy to combat haumai should be to devote oneself to God and not to be attached to objects or people. Neither should one be attached to spiritual achievements. Thus, someone who is devoted to God should not take false pride in that devotion, otherwise this is similar to being attached to haumai.

Insight

Haumai may involve a sense of attachment to any aspects of the material world, including a desire to acquire any material possessions, and placing this in terms of importance above the idea of the spiritual life.

Perhaps the most important element in gaining a true spiritual understanding of God is for the individual to practise meditation upon God's name. Through this process of disciplined meditation the souls of human beings are brought into a unity with the hukam. There are two Panjabi terms that are used for meditation. *Nam simaran* means approximately 'remembering the name of God'. It signifies a form of meditation during which the mind of the Sikh is focused continuously on God. *Nam japan* indicates the meditation process whereby the name of God is repeated over and over again, as in the process of chanting a *mantram*. Both types of meditation have the purpose of calming the mind and making it receptive to the removal of haumai.

Such meditation, if carried out regularly, transforms the individual from being *manmukh* to being *gurmukh*. The former describes a person who is very much orientated towards the rather superficial, materialistic aspects of life; the latter describes the person who is focused very much on God.

The ultimate purpose of the Sikh religious experience is the attainment of a spiritual state known as *sahaj*. This term means approximately 'to merge' or 'to blend' and signifies the process whereby the individual merges his or her spiritual being with God. This is, by its very definition, a mystical process and hence very difficult for humans to describe or convey in mere language. Nevertheless, the sahaj experience is provisionally described as being a state of peace and tranquillity. It is also asserted that being in a state of sahaj provides escape from the cycle of birth and death, in an analogous manner to the process of *moksha* in Hinduism.

Insight

Meditation within Sikhism is designed to enable the individual to reach the state of *sahaj*. As with spiritual goals in religion generally, this state is difficult to describe because of its mystical nature.

Organization

Within Sikhism, the *gurdwara*, or building used for congregational worship, is the centre of religious and community activities. Gurdwaras, like any religious building, differ in structure and plan, but a typical layout would involve the following rooms. Upon entry there will be a small room or alcove for leaving one's outside shoes, since these are not worn within the main part of the gurdwara. There will also, perhaps downstairs, be a communal kitchen and dining room. This is for the institution of the langar. Sikhism grew in a social climate where brahminical Hinduism was the prevalent religious system and this involved considerable ritual practice, particularly in relation to food. People of one caste, particularly the brahmins, would only consume food which had been prepared by the same caste. This type of custom was one way in which social divisions were perpetuated and the Sikh Gurus were particularly opposed to this type of belief system. The langar was a communal meal, the function of which was to demonstrate the equality of all people and to help to break down some of these caste divisions.

Insight

The langar is still an important element in the life of the gurdwara and of the local Sikh community. It provides an opportunity for all members of the community to meet and eat together, irrespective of status or social background.

Upstairs, there will typically be a prayer hall in which is located the *Guru Granth Sahib*. This is the focus of all religious activity and devotion in the gurdwara. The *Guru Granth Sahib* is placed under an ornate frame on top of which is a decorated canopy. This is to indicate the significance of the holy book. In addition, a respected member of the community usually sits behind the holy book, waving a *chawri* or type of fan over it. This is symbolic of the importance of and respect for the *Guru Granth Sahib*. The chawri traditionally consists of strands of yak hair set into a silver handle.

The prayer room is usually carpeted but has no furniture. The members of the congregation sit on the floor, the men sitting separately from the women. Sitting on the floor ensures that everyone sits at a lower level than the *Guru Granth Sahib*, which is again a mark of respect. The separation of men and women does not in any way signify a distinction between the genders in terms of social status within the faith, but is simply related to perceptions of modesty, where men and women might otherwise sit very closely together in a crowded prayer hall. There is great stress throughout the Sikh faith on the equality of all human beings. It is regarded as a respectful act to cover one's head in the prayer hall. If a man is not wearing a *pagri*, or turban, then the norm is to use a cotton handkerchief to place on one's head. This is also usually expected of non-Sikh visitors to a gurdwara.

Neither tobacco nor alcohol should be taken into a gurdwara, as these are regarded as inappropriate substances to have in a religious context.

Within Sikhism there is no established class of priests or clergy and this is again related to the concept of equality of all people within the faith. Nevertheless, there are people who offer themselves to carry out administrative responsibilities within the religion or are perhaps invited to do so because they possess certain skills or knowledge. Most larger gurdwaras have a person designated as the *granthi*, who generally looks after the gurdwara, opening it early in the morning for prayers and looking after the premises. The granthi is also the guardian of the *Guru Granth Sahib*. The gurdwara will also usually have a management committee which takes the kind of management decisions necessary for the continuance of the premises. Sometimes respected individuals may be designated by the term *giani* or *sant*. The former usually implies that the individual possesses considerable knowledge and understanding of the scriptures. The term 'sant' can be reasonably translated as 'saint' and is used for someone commonly regarded as a devout and spiritually minded person.

When members of the congregation enter the prayer hall it is normal to bow to the *Guru Granth Sahib* before taking one's place. The communal worship usually consists of a combination of singing hymns from the *Guru Granth Sahib*, accompanied perhaps by musicians, saying prayers and listening to spiritual talks. Worship may take place on any day of the week but in gurdwaras in England it is perhaps usual to have the main worship on Sundays. As people leave the prayer hall they may be given *karah prasad*, which is a sweet flour paste made from flour, sugar and butter.

It is common after the main congregational worship to have a langar meal. This is offered freely to all Sikhs and to visitors. It is a simple meal, usually consisting of spicy vegetarian food with *chappatis*. It may be paid for from gurdwara funds or a family may sponsor a particular langar and pay for the food themselves.

The gurdwara is very much the community and spiritual focus for the lives of Sikhs, but religious activity does take place in the home also. Devout Sikhs will read the *Guru Granth Sahib* regularly at home and on special occasions there may be an *akhand path*, which is a continuous reading of the entire *Guru Granth Sahib*. Sikhs are very proud of their religious tradition and have managed to sustain it through often adverse circumstances.

Insight

The Gurmukhi script of the *Guru Granth Sahib* is the same as the script used to write modern Panjabi. It is normal for the Sikh community in an area to provide classes in the written and spoken language, in order to sustain understanding among the younger generations.

10 THINGS TO REMEMBER

1 *The Sikh religion evolved in Panjab in India.*

2 *It was founded by Guru Nanak, who was born in 1469* CE *at Talwandi.*

3 *Accompanied by a Muslim named Mardana, Guru Nanak travelled on pilgrimages to a number of holy cities.*

4 *After many years of travelling, Guru Nanak settled at Kartarpur, where he assumed the life of a peasant farmer.*

5 *He constructed a* dharamsala, *a building for the emerging Sikh community.*

6 *There he instituted the* langar, *or communal meal, which symbolized the equality of all people.*

7 *Guru Nanak died in 1539* CE.

8 *After Guru Nanak, there were a further nine Sikh Gurus who extended the foundation of the faith.*

9 *Guru Angad developed the Gurmukhi script in which the holy scriptures of the Sikhs are written.*

10 *Guru Gobind Singh determined that there would be no human Sikh Guru after him, but that the scriptures, henceforth known as the* Guru Granth Sahib, *would be the Guru.*

14

....

New religious movements

In this chapter you will learn about:
- *Paganism*
- *Jehovah's Witnesses*
- *Brahma Kumaris*
- *Rastafarianism.*

For thousands of years, most societies and cultures have tended to have at least some awareness of the existence of other belief systems. Cultures have come into contact with each other through warfare or trade, and interested individuals have often taken the opportunity to learn something of other cultures and religions. Since the advent of electronic communication and globalization, this process has increased rapidly. Through the internet we can now gain photographic and written data on a wide range of religions, small and large, and compare the belief systems of a large number of different faiths.

The internet also provides an opportunity for individuals to contact others of a like mind or with similar beliefs, either to consolidate an existing religious group, or to start a new organization linking people of a similar belief system. Global electronic communication has thus provided the ideal context for the development of minority interest groups within larger faith organizations, and for the inception and evolution of completely new traditions. The term 'new religious movements' is becoming the accepted academic term to describe religious groupings which are generally outside the mainstream traditions, reflect minority viewpoints, and are 'new' to the extent that they have come to notice in their present form in the relatively recent past. The term 'new religious movements' is, however, a complex concept, and requires a little further clarification.

First of all, new religious movements are not necessarily 'new'. They may, for example, represent a version of an ancient tradition, adapted to the contemporary world. An example might be the contemporary version of the Druid tradition. On the other hand, they may be genuinely new belief systems. It is perhaps worth reflecting that all of the major faiths, with which we can associate a specific founding figure, were all 'new religious movements' at one time. In many cases they were regarded with suspicion and dislike by the existing traditions. In some cases members were persecuted by the established faiths or by the political authorities of the time. Many new religions have almost certainly disappeared without trace throughout the centuries, while a tiny number have managed to establish themselves. Sometimes, the terms 'sect' and 'cult' are used in association with new religious movements, although technically it is worth trying to distinguish them. A sect is usually a group which gradually becomes distinguishable from a much larger tradition. It may not completely break away, but usually has sufficient differences of either doctrine or practice to identify it as a separate entity from the main faith. A cult, on the other hand, is usually a small grouping which is independent of other faiths. It may not build upon any existing tradition, but may represent a complete break with previous religious organizations. Some sects and cults are started by, or associated with, a particularly charismatic leader, and may make certain requirements upon members, either in terms of financial contributions or in terms of adherence to a group ethos. In some cases, members of sects or cults have found it difficult to dissociate themselves, if that was their wish, and for that reason the terms have developed something of a pejorative connotation. It should be emphasized, however, that there is nothing inevitably unethical about sects or cults. One might argue, for instance, that in their early stages Buddhism was a sect of Hinduism, and Christianity a sect of Judaism.

Paganism

HISTORY

Paganism is a general term for a loosely connected range of belief systems derived from pre-Christian nature-worship traditions. The term itself is derived from the Latin *paganus*, meaning 'a person who lives and works in the countryside'. By connotation, the term thus described the religions, belief systems and cultures of those people who lived in more isolated areas, and who had not come under the influence of the newly evolving Christian faith. Early Christians adopted the term to refer to those ancient, pre-Christian traditions from which they wished to distinguish themselves. As Christianity became more and more established, the term 'pagan' was used in a rather pejorative sense, to refer to what were perceived as less-sophisticated, rural beliefs and practices. Even worse, those adhering to pagan beliefs were persecuted and even exterminated, as in the persecution of witches in medieval times. Pagan religions were sometimes seen as a challenge to the developing orthodoxy of Christianity.

One might therefore attempt a rather loose definition of paganism as being those pre-Christian religions indigenous to Europe. This would include, for example, the Druid religion, other traditions associated with the Celts, the Scandinavian traditions associated with the worship of Odin and Thor, and varied shamanic traditions. Such pagan traditions would also have much in common with the indigenous religions of, say, North America, Africa and Australasia. All of these faith traditions would share a sense of the importance of the natural world. In contemporary times, attempts

have been made to recapture the essence of these ancient belief
systems, and to adapt them to the conditions of modern society.
Such practices are sometimes designated 'neo-paganism'.

BELIEF SYSTEM

As indicated above, pagan traditions are varied and can derive
from different geographical areas. Nevertheless, one can discern
several broad commonalities between them. A general but
important issue is that pagan faiths do not view the human being
as being central to the planning or meaning of the universe. There
is a strong pre-eminent belief in the significance of the natural
world, and that human beings are simply a part of that natural
system. There is a general belief in the spiritual element of the
natural world. The latter is seen as a manifestation of a divine
spirit, which may be gender-neutral, or represent both genders,
or be specifically female, as in the case of a Mother Goddess. This
approach to gender, which contrasts somewhat with the largely
male-oriented organizations in established faiths, has led to a
strong sense of gender equality in neo-paganism.

> **Insight**
>
> It is perhaps not surprising that religious systems which have
> evolved over a number of millennia are often associated
> with belief in a spiritual world that is part of the natural
> environment. Religion is perceived as an essential element of
> the natural world around us.

There is also a feeling within paganism of tolerance towards other
faiths. Perhaps partly because of the diversity of practices within
paganism, there is little sense of one approach being absolutely
correct. Paganism tends therefore to be generally inclusive of other
systems, rather than exclusive. This view is also reflected in the
ethical systems of paganism and neo-paganism. There tends not to
be a rigid or prescriptive list of ethical principles. There is usually
simply the overriding principle that anything is permitted, as long
as it does not cause harm to anyone else. The importance of nature

leads also, perhaps not surprisingly, to a preferred use of natural or herbal remedies for illness.

In pre-Christian times it was the norm for religious traditions to be oral in nature, and hence we tend not to have written sources from which to reconstruct patterns of ceremony or ritual. The systematic persecution of pagan faiths during the Christian era often led to the destruction of any existing written source materials. Neo-pagans, therefore, need to establish new patterns of worship based on the best interpretation of any existing traditions or accounts. Wiccans or witches tend to celebrate festivals at the solstices and equinoxes. Further examples of the variation in paganism are provided by Druids who are generally polytheistic, while shamans are often mystical by nature, with no unified pattern of worship.

ORGANIZATION

It is perhaps inherent in the nature of pagan belief that many individuals prefer to practise on their own, and relate to the natural world in an individual way. However, others like the support of organizations and a number of such bodies exist to provide a structured framework and also to act as advocates for pagan beliefs. The Pagan Federation, founded in 1971, acts in relation to pagans in general, while the British Druid Order, established in 1979, represents Druids. It is perhaps worth noting that in some cases pagan organizations are, in effect, reconstituted forms of organizations which would have existed many years ago, and were historically persecuted, suppressed or outlawed. Patterns of religious organization are being recreated for contemporary times, often without a detailed understanding of the original structures.

Insight

In the case of the major world religions, forms of worship including, for example, prayers, hymns, chanting and the reading of scripture are well established. There is generally, however, no such continuity in paganism, and such forms are having to be redeveloped.

Jehovah's Witnesses

HISTORY

The history of the Jehovah's Witnesses movement can be traced to the work of Charles Taze Russell who was born in Pennsylvania in 1852. He initially established a small Bible study group, and gradually developed a personal interest and belief in the idea of the 'second coming' of Jesus. Russell had been a member of the Congregational Church but, as his organization expanded, he decided to formalize it as the 'Zion's Watchtower Tract Society' in 1881. He also summarized his thoughts on religion in the book *Studies in the Scriptures*. In 1931 the name Jehovah's Witnesses was first employed by the organization. The name derives from the Book of Isaiah, in which people are called as witnesses to confirm a belief in Jehovah as the true God.

During the period of Russell's leadership, and also during that of his successors, various predictions have been made for an apocalyptic end to the world, combined with the second coming of Christ. The broad belief was that the world would be largely destroyed and the only survivors would be those who believed in the true doctrines of the Jehovah's Witnesses. For those who were genuine believers an ideal existence of paradise would be established on Earth, in which there would be no pain or suffering, and people would live forever. Such an apocalyptic event has never materialized and, instead, Jehovah's Witnesses developed the related doctrine that Christ had actually returned to Earth, but in a spiritual form only.

BELIEF SYSTEM

The starting point for the beliefs of Jehovah's Witnesses is that Jehovah is the absolute divinity, and that the Bible is the source of religious knowledge. The beliefs of Jehovah's Witnesses are firmly based on the teachings of the Bible. Members of the movement are continuously encouraged to read the Bible, and to use it as a source of wisdom and advice when people are faced with problems or uncertainty. The particular translation of the Bible that is used uniformly is 'The New World Translation' which was produced in 1961. There is a belief among Jehovah's Witnesses that the world will only exist as we know it for a finite time. It will end in a form of apocalypse or Armageddon, after which only devout Jehovah's Witnesses will survive. They will then live in a form of paradise on Earth. There is a deep commitment to spread the news of Jehovah, and to encourage new members. Jehovah's Witnesses are well-known for their efforts to call at people's homes and to convey their beliefs and their optimism in their faith. They have a very strong belief in the significance of the family, and in the way in which the traditional values of the family support both the individual and society. They are strongly pacifist, and will not participate in violent acts or warfare. The religious and spiritual are central to their lives, and they have little interest in the political dimension to society. Jehovah's Witnesses are also well known for not accepting blood transfusions.

ORGANIZATION

Jehovah's Witnesses have a clearly organized administration, which involves the devolution of authority from the headquarters of the movement in Brooklyn, New York.

The principal decision-making agency is the Governing Body, which determines all key questions of what should count as orthodox belief. This body also decides all the important general matters of organizational policy. It controls all the publications of the organization, and in particular those that disseminate the teachings. Importantly too, the Governing Body administers and oversees the publication of *The Watchtower*, the main journal of Jehovah's Witnesses. The main meeting place for the local congregation is the Kingdom Hall. From here, individuals commit themselves to going from house to house to pass on their faith and belief system.

Brahma Kumaris

HISTORY

The Brahma Kumaris were established in 1936 under the spiritual
influence and leadership of Dada Lekhraj, a man who experienced
a series of religious visions and who transmitted his ideas to
the small religious group of which he was a part. This group of
spiritually-minded people was based in Hyderabad, in what is now
Pakistan, and originally had the name Om Mandali. They were
interested in trying to gain a better spiritual understanding of the
world, living a life devoted to spirituality and meditation.

Dada Lekhraj was named Lekhraj Kripilani at birth in 1876, and
was brought up in a Hindu family. Most of his life he worked in
business and was very successful, becoming, by the age of 60, very
wealthy. It was around this time, in 1936, that he started having
visions while meditating. Later, he assumed the name of Brahma
Baba. He died in 1969. The group that he founded moved first to
Karachi, and then in 1950 to Mount Abu in Rajasthan, India. The
organization is now officially known by its full title of the 'Brahma
Kumaris World Spiritual University' and has approximately one
million members.

BELIEF SYSTEM

The overall approach of the Brahma Kumaris is to encourage
people to focus much more on spiritual questions rather than on
the materialism which tends to be a prevalent feature of Western
society. It tends to do this by advocating a form of meditation
linked to the principles of Raja yoga. As in many Eastern traditions,
one of the central purposes of meditation is to calm the mind and to
lead to a tranquil approach to life. For Brahma Kumaris meditation
leads to an enhanced state of knowledge or understanding of
the self. There is a belief in the existence of a human soul which
is a separate entity from the physical body. The soul potentially
exists forever, and Brahma Kumaris believe in the concept of

reincarnation. There is a belief in principles of living which are
similar to those espoused by classical Hinduism and Buddhism, for
example, peaceful cooperation with others, non-violence towards
the living world, a vegetarian diet and regular periods of meditation.

ORGANIZATION

The World Headquarters of the movement at Mount Abu are
concerned with the overall management and administration of the
organization. It is here that key decisions are taken about policy
or questions concerning religious matters. The organization has
an international office in London, which oversees to some extent
the work of the Brahma Kumaris in approximately 7,000 centres
around the world, in around 90 countries. There are approaching
one million members or students of the Brahma Kumaris World
Spiritual University. One feature of the organization is the strong
emphasis upon gender equality, particularly in terms of those
who occupy senior administrative positions. This clearly reflects
the original views of Brahma Baba who, as long ago as 1937,
formed a committee composed of eight women to administer the
organization. The following year, Brahma Baba established a trust
fund which was to be administered by this committee, and donated
all his wealth and possessions to that trust. To this day, women
still predominate in the running of the Brahma Kumaris.

Rastafarianism

HISTORY

Fundamentally, Rastafarianism has its roots in the history of the
African slave trade, and with the impulse of some black people
to return to an idealized homeland in Africa. This idea was given
expression in the teachings of the Jamaican, Marcus Garvey (1887–
1940), who not only wanted black people to return to their roots
in Africa, but also wanted them to dissociate themselves completely
from white culture, and to take a pride in a distinctive black

culture. While the movement is much associated with Jamaica, it has latterly spread across the globe, especially through the influence and popularity of reggae music, with which it is connected.

The Rastafarian movement had no distinctive figurehead until the crowning of Haile Selassie as Emperor of Ethiopia in 1930. From that point on, he became a form of symbol of the Rastafarian movement, and came to represent the desire of black people to return to Africa. Indeed Ethiopia became a symbolic representation of Heaven on Earth. Haile Selassie travelled to Jamaica on 21 April 1966, and this has since been a special commemorative date within the movement. He died in 1975 but he has remained the symbolic figure of Rastafarianism.

Insight

The idea of returning to Africa may be a rather utopian and idealistic ambition. It is perhaps more important as a metaphor, or for what it represents, rather than being a widespread real desire to live in Africa.

During the 1960s Rastafarians were associated with protest movements in Jamaica against black poverty and black exploitation worldwide. However, even though a political dimension to Rastafarianism was developing, there still remained a major thread within the movement which was basically spiritual and religious, rather than aiming for political change. Nevertheless, in the public consciousness, rightly or wrongly, the movement became associated to some extent with the movement for 'black power'. From the 1970s onwards, the popularity of Bob Marley and reggae music had a considerable effect upon the public awareness of the movement worldwide. People generally became more widely conscious of the philosophy and ideals of the movement.

Insight

The combination of a religious dimension with political action in relation to race is found in other groups such as the Nation of Islam, which is particularly associated with the name of Malcolm X.

BELIEF SYSTEM

Rastafarianism has developed its own distinctive terminology and conceptual system. One of the central concepts is that of 'Babylon'. Perhaps taken originally from the notion of the Jews exiled in Babylon and subject to oppression by the conquerors, Babylon as a term has come to represent the oppression of black people by white society. Clearly dating back to the slave trade, in more recent times the term represents all ways in which black people are perceived to have been oppressed by whites. Black culture is seen as having been not only devalued but almost eliminated by slavery, and by subsequent economic and political suppression. Black people are perceived as being disadvantaged economically, and in other respects such as education, by the white domination of society. The values of the old colonial society are seen as still existing in contemporary society.

'Jah' is the name for God used by Rastafarians. Haile Selassie is seen as having represented a form of divinity on Earth, and Ethiopia as an earthly Heaven. The latter is also referred to as 'Zion'. Haile Selassie is often represented figuratively as a lion, or as the 'Lion of Judah'. This is not unconnected with the habit of growing the hair into 'dreadlocks': on the one hand dreadlocks represent an image of the lion; on the other, the growing of the hair is also a gesture against the conventions of hairstyle and appearance in white society.

Notwithstanding the association with black power, the fundamental belief of the movement is one of non-violence. This is manifested in several ways, but primarily by a preference for a vegetarian lifestyle. Rastafarians tend to prefer vegetarian food grown in an organic way, and do not drink stimulants such as coffee or alcohol. They do, however, smoke marijuana (ganga), although within the purist Rastafarian tradition this is used only within religious events. There is a general difficulty with defining precisely the teachings and belief system of Rastafarianism, and this is partly connected with the lack of a clear organizational hierarchy and system for specifying agreed doctrines.

ORGANIZATION

The lack of a precise organization is almost certainly connected with the way in which personal freedom is valued by Rastafarians. The esteem in which personal autonomy is held may in turn be connected with the sense of oppression felt by black people in the face of 'white' economic and political structures. There are however, informal gatherings which have a distinctly spiritual flavour. There are informal meetings which arise when a group of people wish to discuss issues. These may start with some form of religious statement or prayer, and be followed by the ritual smoking of ganga. Community celebrations or dances are also held, particularly on days celebrating key events in the lives of Marcus Garvey or Haile Selassie. In comparison with many faiths, however, there are no accepted teachings or doctrines, no regular use of ritual or ceremony, and no religious hierarchy.

10 THINGS TO REMEMBER

1 'New religious movements' is a term used for minority faiths outside the mainstream traditions.

2 A sect is a group which breaks away from a much larger religious tradition.

3 A cult is a new religious group which tends to have developed more autonomously, and may not have any clear links with mainstream groups.

4 Pagan religions were originally those that remained outside the influence of early Christianity.

5 Pagan traditions share a sense of the importance of the natural world.

6 Jehovah's Witnesses believe in the religious authority of the Bible, and in Jehovah as the supreme divinity.

7 Brahma Kumaris stress the spiritual as opposed to the materialistic dimension to life.

8 They advocate the use of meditation techniques linked to Raja Yoga.

9 Rastafarianism owes much to the teachings of Marcus Garvey (1887–1940).

10 The late Haile Selassie, Emperor of Ethiopia, became a figurehead for the Rastafarian movement.

15

Conclusion: the future of religion

In this chapter you will learn about:
- *the nature of a multi-faith society*
- *the development of 'secular' religions.*

One of the most interesting recent developments in world faiths, which began to take place from around the end of World War II, has been the enormous diffusion of different religions across the world. Most of this happened because of post-war migration and resettlement, but, in addition, there has been the effect of television and latterly the internet, which has resulted in a much widened consciousness of different faiths around the world.

Many countries, including Britain, are now multicultural, multi-ethnic and multi-faith societies. From being a mono-religious society, albeit one with different denominations, Britain has become a multi-faith society and this trend has been mirrored in many other countries. People nowadays have a choice of faith, which was in effect lacking in previous generations. We are now aware of competing value systems and religious practices, with which only perhaps a minority of people were previously familiar. The cultures associated with other faiths have also had an impact upon society.

Insight
One of the consequences of people being exposed to a variety of belief systems is that they are free to select elements of spirituality from different religions, which can have an effect upon their original faith.

An example of this has perhaps been the influence of the doctrine of non-violence, which is particularly characteristic of religions that have developed on the Indian subcontinent. In the decades leading up to the Independence of India in 1947, Mahatma Gandhi and his fellow political activists were able to use the Hindu doctrine of *ahimsa*, or non-violence, to support a particular form of peaceful demonstration. They sought not to confront the British but to use this particular religious doctrine as the basis for peaceful marches and demonstrations, which proved to be highly effective. Such demonstrations became the models for many subsequent such political actions in the West. Young people, particularly, saw in non-violent action a means of effectively demonstrating against a society or government, while at the same time adopting what many would regard as a morally acceptable strategy.

Insight

Mahatma Gandhi and, later, Martin Luther King showed the effectiveness of non-violent methods in changing society. While not totally successful, they managed through such methods to alter society's general receptiveness to a more egalitarian approach.

The migration of Hindus to many countries around the world brought their culture and faith within reach of many who had never been to the Indian subcontinent. In the UK, Hindu communities in such places as Leicester established large Hindu temples which became centres for sustaining the faith in a new country. The principle of non-violence has also been disseminated by Jains, Buddhists and Quakers.

The idea of non-violence has also influenced, to some extent, the movement for vegetarianism. Buddhists are not under a strict obligation to be vegetarian but, generally perhaps, tend to be so. Many groups of Hindus are vegetarian, although their religion generally may not exclude them from eating some forms of meat.

The advent of a multi-faith society in, say, Britain and North America has certainly enriched society and brought people in general into contact with a wide variety of customs and cultures.

In many societies, social customs in general are very much connected with the religion that is being practised. There is thus an intimate connection between the religious and the social and secular, which is not as obvious in Western secular society.

In Britain, for example, people have become familiar with the fact that Muslims fast during Ramadan. Teachers who teach Muslim students have become aware of, and try to be sensitive to, the pressures that this fasting places upon the students. The cultures of other societies have become evident in British society in many different ways, whether it be through the availability of food from other countries, an awareness of why people from different cultures wear particular kinds of clothes, or the familiar sight in our towns of temples and mosques with the external appearance of buildings from Eastern countries.

There can be little doubt that this contact with people from other countries and cultures has widened the cultural awareness of indigenous people and in some cases it has initiated sufficient interest for them to subscribe to a faith that is relatively new to this country. It may still not be very common, but neither is it particularly unusual to find English people who have become Buddhists or Muslims or who have joined a Hindu group or denomination.

Insight

Exposure to other cultures and religions has probably had a considerably liberalizing effect upon society, in that multicultural awareness encourages a sense of tolerance towards others.

There is no doubt that there is something of an imbalance between the numbers of British people who may claim to be nominally Christian and those who actually attend church or participate in some active manner in Christian life and worship. One may conjecture why this is so, but it is not easy to draw any conclusions that can be substantiated. There is almost certainly a multiplicity of factors.

It seems a reasonable hypothesis that as the nature of society changes, so too will the nature of religious practice. Religion is part of society and there will almost inevitably be a dynamic interaction between the two. We might reasonably argue that in the historical period up to the Industrial Revolution in Europe, there was a very strong sense of social cohesion built around a rural, agrarian culture. In such a society religious belief was a potent force, providing one of the major unifying factors in society. Human beings had relatively few opportunities to exercise their individualism and yet this was compensated for by the sense of solidarity and cohesion in society.

With the advent of the Industrial Revolution there was initiated a period of increased movement for people, as they were able to work in different locations, rather than in the same rural area as had always been the case. A period of rapidly increasing individualism began. People were able to make far more decisions for themselves and also to make choices about the particular world view to which they would subscribe. No doubt, though, there were also disadvantages to the new social structure in terms of the reduced sense of social cohesion. As we come to contemporary times, there is clearly an enormously increased individualism in society and one might hypothesize that this has been one factor in a reduced interest in a single state religion and an expanding interest in a multiplicity of other faiths and religious sects and, indeed, what we might term 'secular religions' such as yoga.

Insight

We often hear it suggested that the world today is increasingly secular, and people are less interested in religion. It may be, however, that people are interested in different forms of spiritual expression, and in types of expression that are more individualistic and less part of religious organizations.

To follow this hypothesis further, one could argue that people are beginning to exercise their individualism in terms of belief systems and religions in much the same way in which they exercise it in other areas of life. Mass communications and the internet have made people much more aware of other cultures. In addition, greatly enhanced travel opportunities have enabled people to travel on 'package tours' to areas of the globe that until recently were regarded as 'remote'. Moreover, these are often areas where travellers learn about other faiths and belief systems. When they return to their home country, they sometimes follow up the interest.

The exercise of individualism may also result in people exploring small religious groups or sects. The latter term is sometimes used in a pejorative sense, although this may not be appropriate. It should be remembered that some mainstream religions have started off as a 'sect', in the sense of a minority, unorthodox viewpoint. Later they have become more popular and gradually gained a wider acceptance.

People may be attracted to religious sects for a variety of reasons, including the originality of their doctrines, the apparently more informal nature of their organization and perhaps the charismatic nature of the leadership. Some religious groups which commenced as sects, such as the Quakers, or Society of Friends, founded by George Fox and the Mormons, or Church of Jesus Christ of Latter-day Saints, have grown and acquired a sense of orthodoxy, even if they are not counted among the largest mainstream Christian denominations. Other sects – for example, that founded by Bhagwan Rajneesh, based on a form of meditation – do not appear to have been accepted as orthodox, while nevertheless attracting interest.

During the last few decades, religious fundamentalism has attracted a number of followers. The term 'fundamentalism' is perhaps most commonly used in the context of Christianity and Islam, but it can easily be applied to any religious tradition. As a philosophy it tends to rely upon the more literal interpretation of scriptural sources, and to look back historically to a period in society when there was perhaps more social solidarity, conformity to agreed norms and values, and a perhaps stricter adherence to scripture. To some extent such a historical period may never have existed, but it may still be very real in the consciousness of followers. Fundamentalists tend to see contemporary society as too individualistic and too materialistic. They often prefer to have a greater involvement of organized religion within the secular state. Fundamentalists feel that this provides a more moral society. Although such a system provides less freedom and autonomy of action for the individual, fundamentalists consider that this is a price worth paying for a society with more clearly defined, spiritual values.

There is also a sustained interest in what we might term secular religions or traditions which, while having a spiritual element, are generally practised within a largely secular environment, and without an overtly religious approach. The practice of meditation can be carried out in a purely secular manner, almost as a form of psychotherapy. It may help to calm the mind and to reduce stress, without being seen as part of any faith or belief system. The interest in yoga is very widespread and can be purely on the level of treating it as a form of physical exercise which helps to maintain the muscles in a supple and relaxed state. Accompanied by yogic breathing exercises, it too is a form of meditation and may be beneficial in reducing stress and calming the mind.

There are thus no signs that human beings do not continue to be impelled by the spiritual quest, yet in contemporary society they have far more means at their disposal for trying to resolve the great religious questions to their personal satisfaction. There are no longer great social pressures to subscribe to a single view of religion. People are able to select from a wide variety of different traditions, each eager for their attention.

It may well be that no matter how materialistic the world becomes, at certain points in their lives people will still turn within themselves, searching for answers to questions that have been part of the human condition for millennia.

There may be more and more organizations offering answers, but the great spiritual questions of humanity remain.

10 THINGS TO REMEMBER

1 *Population movements across the world since World War II have created contacts between different religions.*

2 *Many countries have become multi-faith societies.*

3 *In some cases this has led to people converting to a religion from another culture.*

4 *The religious principle of non-violence has influenced forms of political action.*

5 *Vegetarianism has been linked to the philosophy of non-violence.*

6 *Recent years have seen an expansion in new religious movements.*

7 *Alternative forms of spirituality such as yoga and meditation have become popular.*

8 *The concept of religious fundamentalism is much discussed, without an adequate definition necessarily emerging.*

9 *It is not uncommon for people to claim membership of a faith, without participating actively.*

10 *The increased availability of inexpensive travel has opened up a range of religions to people, and broadened understanding of other faiths.*

Glossary

Abu Bakr In Islam, he was the first caliph, after the death of Muhammad.

ahimsa (or non-violence) An approach to the spiritual life advocated by many religious groups, but perhaps most specifically associated with Jains and also Mahatma Gandhi. Jains, for example, will sometimes sweep the path ahead of them with a small brush in order to avoid stepping on small creatures.

Ahura Mazda The deity worshipped in Zoroastrianism.

Amaterasu The most influential *kami* in Shinto and the goddess of the sun.

Amritsar The holy city for Sikhs in Panjab. The so-called Golden Temple is located at Amritsar.

anapanasati A form of Buddhist meditation which involves focusing the attention on the steady inhaling and exhaling of the breath, in order to try to calm the mind.

Anglican Communion The churches located in different parts of the world that share matters of doctrine and worship with the Church of England.

Ark The container in a Jewish synagogue in which are kept the Torah scrolls.

ashramas In classical Hindu tradition, the life of an individual Hindu is ideally expected to fall into four stages or *ashramas*.

Asoka Became the ruler of most of the Indian subcontinent in 268 BCE, and later converted to Buddhism. After his conversion, he attempted to rule India according to Buddhist principles.

Avesta The Zoroastrian scriptural texts.

Baha'i faith The faith founded by Baha'ullah.

Baha'ullah (or Mirza Husayn Ali Nuri) A religious teacher who was influenced by the Bab and who founded the Baha'i faith.

Benares A city in India on the River Ganges, which is very holy to Hindus. It was also just outside Benares, at the Deer Park, that the Buddha delivered his first sermon.

Bhagavad Gita One of the best-known scriptures of Hinduism. It is a component of the Hindu epic, the *Mahabharata*.

bhikkhu A Buddhist monk.

Bodhidharma The Indian Buddhist monk who in the early sixth century CE took to China the ideas that formed the basis of Ch'an Buddhism and then later Zen Buddhism as found in Japan.

bodhisattva A concept in Mahayana Buddhism. A *bodhisattva* is an individual who has the capacity to attain enlightenment, but chooses to remain outside nirvana in order to help others achieve enlightenment.

Brahma Kumaris A religious group advocating meditation and Raja yoga.

Buddhism The religion initiated by Siddhartha Gautama, who was known later as the Buddha, or 'enlightened one'.

caste Classical Hindu society was divided into four main social strata termed castes. The castes were the *brahmins* or priests; the *kshatriyas* or warriors; the *vaishyas* or merchants; and the *shudras* or manual labourers.

Ch'an Buddhism A form of Buddhism that evolved in China, which emphasizes meditation practice. In Japan, it was the precursor of Zen Buddhism.

Church of England The 'established' Church in England.

Confucianism A Chinese religious philosophy founded by K'ung Fu-tzu, or Confucius, who lived approximately from 551 BCE to 479 BCE. For over 2,000 years the principles of Confucianism were accepted as the basis of social and political organization in China.

Council of Chalcedon Held in 451 CE, it established four centres for the Christian Orthodox Church at Constantinople, Jerusalem, Alexandria and Antioch.

creed A succinct statement of doctrinal belief, as in the Apostles' Creed and Nicene Creed in Christianity.

cult A new religious group which tends to have developed autonomously, and may not have any clear links with mainstream groups.

Dalai Lama The spiritual leader of Tibetan Buddhism.

dhikr A form of spiritual meditation in Sufism, which involves 'remembering' the name of God, over and over again.

Digambara A school of Jains who traditionally do not wear any clothes.

dukkha (or suffering) One of the central concepts in Buddhism. It emphasizes the unsatisfactory nature of the world. The main message of Buddhism is that suffering can be reduced by adherence to the teaching of the Buddha.

Eid ul-Adha The festival marking the conclusion of the *Hajj* for Muslims.

Eid ul-Fitr The festival at the conclusion of Ramadan, when there is a celebration and presents are exchanged.

Five Pillars of Islam The five principal duties that Muslims are expected to fulfil as part of the faith.

Gandhi Mahatma Gandhi was a lawyer and social activist, who in his political campaigns consistently applied the principles of non-violence.

Gayatri Mantram A short religious verse from the *Rig Veda*, used by Hindus as a *mantram*.

General Synod The principal decision-making body of the Church of England. It is divided into three 'Houses': the House of Laity, the House of Clergy and the House of Bishops.

gurdwara In Sikhism, the building used for congregational worship.

Gurmukhi The script used for writing the *Guru Granth Sahib* in the Sikh religion. It was developed by Guru Angad.

guru This term may have several different, but related meanings in different traditions. In Hinduism, it means a religious teacher or spiritual guide. In Sikhism, it may mean one of the ten human Gurus. Within Sikhism, it may also mean the spiritual Absolute or God; and it may also mean the holy book of the Sikhs, the *Guru Granth Sahib*.

Guru Arjan The Sikh Guru who compiled the *Adi Granth* or *Guru Granth Sahib*, the holy scripture of the Sikhs.

Guru Gobind Singh The last of the ten Sikh Gurus. After Gobind Singh, the *Guru Granth Sahib* became the Guru.

haiku Short Japanese poems which often reflect Buddhist themes.

Hajj The pilgrimage to Mecca. It is the duty of all Muslims to make the *Hajj* pilgrimage at least once during their lives.

hatha yoga The branch of yoga which is concerned with the practice of postures or *asanas*.

haumai Within Sikhism, this is regarded as one of the main obstacles to attaining salvation. It is approximately translated as 'self-interest' or 'self-centredness'.

Hijra In Islam, this is the escape of the early Muslim community from Mecca to Medina in 622 CE.

Hinduism The original religion of India, from about the beginning of the second millennium BCE onwards. At about this time, migrating people known as Aryans invaded India from the Asian steppes.

I Ching (or *Book of Changes*) One of the so-called five classics of Confucianism. It purports to provide ways of predicting the future through the interpretation of patterns of hexagrams.

impermanence A central concept in Buddhism. Buddhists try to focus on the temporary nature of the world, both animate and inanimate. They try to use this understanding to become non-attached to the world.

Jainism An Indian religion founded by the sage Vardhamana, or as he is usually known, Mahavira.

Jehovah's Witnesses A religious group with a strong belief in the Bible and Jehovah.

Kaaba The large cube-shaped building located in the Grand Mosque in Mecca. Pilgrims on the *Hajj* walk around the *Kaaba* seven times, in an anti-clockwise direction.

Kabbalah The mystical tradition within Judaism.

kami The spiritual entities that derive from the universal spirit as seen in Shinto. They may be present in distinguished human beings or ancestors, in natural objects such as rivers or trees or in mythological characters.

karma The doctrine in Hinduism that when people behave ethically or unethically, they will gain appropriate consequences for their actions.

Khalsa The community of initiated Sikhs.

koan An enigmatic saying which is used as part of meditation practice in the Rinzai school of Zen Buddhism. The individual is asked to reflect on and analyse the koan during meditation.

Kusinagara The town near to which the Buddha died.

langar In Sikh tradition, this is the communal meal served at the gurdwara. It helps to emphasize the unity of humanity.

Mahavira The name of the founder of Jainism. He lived from approximately 599 BCE to 527 BCE.

Mahayana (or Great Vehicle) The school of Buddhism that developed in China, Tibet and Japan.

mantram A syllable or short group of syllables which are of religious significance in Hinduism, repeated as an aid to meditation.

Martin Luther (1483 CE to 1546 CE) A German theologian who was one of the major figures of the Reformation. He is famously said to have fixed his 95 theses to the door of the church in Wittenberg.

Middle Way A term often used for the Buddha's teaching, signifying a balance between asceticism and materialism.

moksha A Hindu term which signifies release from the endless cycle of birth and rebirth.

mosque (or *masjid*) Traditionally the building where Muslims gather for prayer.

Muhammad Regarded by Muslims as the prophet of Islam, who received a series of spiritual revelations from God. Muhammad was born in 570 CE and died in 632 CE.

Nam simaran A form of meditation in Sikhism which means approximately 'remembering the name of God'.

Noble Eightfold Path In Buddhism, the teaching of the Buddha by which means people can gradually reduce suffering.

no-self A doctrine in Buddhism that there is no permanent soul or self which can continue in existence after the death of the individual.

paganism A connected group of belief systems with a strong affiliation with nature.

Panj Pyare (or Five Beloved Ones) The original five members of the Sikh *Khalsa*.

Parsis Zoroastrians originally from Iran who migrated to India and settled in the Bombay area.

Passover (or *Pesach*) The Jewish festival which commemorates the escape of the Israelite people from servitude in Egypt, as recounted in the Book of Exodus.

pranayama Breathing exercises used in yoga.

Qur'an The holy book of Islam, which contains the revelations received by Muhammad.

Rajagrha The location of the First Council of Buddhists, held after the Buddha's death, in order, among other things, to consolidate and agree in a standard form, the Buddha's teaching.

Ramadan The ninth month of the Islamic calendar, during which adult Muslims are required to fast from sunrise to sunset.

Ramakrishna A famous Bengali mystic, who argued for the essential unity of all religions.

Rastafarianism A group associated with the return of black people to their roots in Africa, and with a non-violent and vegetarian lifestyle.

Rinzai A school of Zen Buddhism that uses the koan as part of the discipline of meditation practice.

Sabbath The day of the week set aside by Jews for rest and prayer.

sadhu A wandering religious mendicant, or *sannyasin* in Hinduism.

sahaj In Sikhism, this is the spiritual condition which is the ultimate aim of the faith. It means approximately 'to merge' and signifies the merging or blending of the individual spiritual being with God.

salat (or ritual prayer) The requirement that, five times a day, Muslims should pray in a certain manner while facing in the direction of Mecca.

sangha The community of Buddhist monks and nuns.

sannyasin In Hinduism, a wandering religious mendicant. The term is also used for the fourth and final *ashrama* or stage of life in classical Hinduism.

Sanskrit The language of classical Hinduism.

satori The name used for the enlightenment experience in Zen Buddhism.

Sayyid Ali Muhammad (the Bab) A religious teacher born in Iran, who was an influence on the development of Baha'ism.

sect A group which breaks away from a much larger religious tradition.

Sermon of the Turning of the Wheel of the Law The name of the first sermon delivered by the Buddha at the Deer Park at Sarnath near Benares in India. In it the Buddha enunciated the principles of the Four Noble Truths and the Noble Eightfold Path.

Shahada (or Profession of Faith) This is the summary statement of what it means to be a Muslim. The statement is: 'There is no god but the God and Muhammad is the messenger of the God.'

Shema One of the principal prayers in Judaism, affirming some of the basic tenets of the faith.

Shinto The original religion of Japan before the advent of Buddhism. A traditional feature of Shinto is that it emphasizes a love of the natural world.

Shoghi Effendi The last leader of Baha'ism, before the transition to an elected body called the House of Justice, to administer the religion.

Sikhism The religion founded in Panjab in northern India by Guru Nanak, who was born in 1469 CE.

Soto Zen A school of Zen Buddhism founded by Dogen.

Sufism The mystical tradition in Islam.

Svetambara A school within Jainism that considers it a sufficient mark of asceticism to wear simple white robes.

synagogue The building used for communal prayer in Judaism.

tai chi A form of exercise characteristic of Taoism. It consists of a series of gentle postures, combined with breathing exercises.

Talmud One of the principal religious texts of Judaism. It consists of commentaries written by rabbis on religious matters and Jewish law. There are two Talmuds, one written in Babylon and the other in Jerusalem.

tao In Taoism, the spiritual energy present throughout the universe. The term is also used to describe the 'way' or discipline which should be followed by an aspirant who wishes to attain a mystical union with the *tao*.

Taoism A Chinese religion which is assumed to have been founded by a sage named Lao Tzu in about the fourth century BCE. The purpose of the religion is to become united with the *tao* or spiritual force which pervades the universe.

Tao Te Ching The principal religious text of Taoism.

tefillin Leather boxes Jewish men wear on the forehead and arm when praying. The boxes contain extracts from the scriptures.

Theravada (or Way of the Elders) The branch of Buddhism that developed in Sri Lanka and South-east Asia. The religious texts of the Theravada are written in Pali.

tirthankaras Enlightened spiritual teachers in the Jain tradition.

Torah One of the principal religious texts of Judaism which consists of the first five books of the Old Testament.

torii The entrance to a Shinto shrine in Japan.

Towers of Silence The towers found in the Bombay area of India, in which Parsis dispose of their dead. They do so by leaving the corpses exposed to the sky, whereupon they are consumed by vultures.

Trinity A doctrinal term in Christianity which signifies God as the Father, God as the Son and God as the Holy Ghost or Holy Spirit.

upanayana (or second birth) The ceremony at which a Hindu boy from one of the first three castes is invested with the *yajnopavita* or sacred thread.

Upanishads Mystical Hindu texts written from about 600 BCE onwards. They speak of the ideal of the ascetic, meditative life and of the individual who desires to unite the individual human soul with the universal soul of *Brahman*.

vihara The name given to a Buddhist monastery.

vinaya The code of conduct of Buddhist monks and nuns.

vipassana A form of Buddhist meditation sometimes known as 'insight' meditation. During this type of meditation, the individual tries to reflect upon the thoughts which come and go in the mind.

Vivekananda A Hindu teacher who attended the World Parliament of Religions in 1893 CE and who advocated a synthesis of Western and Hindu thought.

wu-wei A central concept of Taoism. It consists of the apparent paradox of action through non-action or acting in an apparently effortless manner through being in a delicate equilibrium with one's environment.

yin and **yang** Two related but opposing ideas of Chinese religion and philosophy. *Yin* is the passive element and *yang* the active element, inherent in the nature of existence.

yoga In Hinduism, a means of achieving salvation. The word is related to the word 'yoke', and signifies the joining together of the individual soul and the universal soul of *Brahman*.

Yom Kippur The Jewish 'Day of Atonement' when people seek the forgiveness of God for the wrong deeds they feel they have committed during the past year.

zakat The giving of alms to charitable causes, required of all Muslims. The *zakat* is normally about two and a half per cent of an individual's income.

Zen The distinctive form of Buddhism found in Japan. Zen places great emphasis on the practice of meditation.

Zoroastrianism An ancient religion of Iran which was founded by Zoroaster, or Zarathustra, who lived in approximately 1500 BCE.

Taking it further

Further reading

Armstrong, K. (1994) *A History of God*. London, Random House.

Barber, R. (1991) *Pilgrimages*. Woodbridge, Boydell.

Beckerlegge, G. ed. (1998) *The World Religions Reader*. London, Routledge.

Boyce, M. (1988) *Zoroastrians: Their Religious Beliefs and Practices*. London, Routledge.

Bruce, S. (1995) *Religion in Modern Britain*. Oxford, Oxford University Press.

Bruce, S. (1996) *Religion in the Modern World*. Oxford, Oxford University Press.

Castelli, E.A. ed. (2001) *Women, Gender, Religion: A Reader*. New York, Palgrave.

Cohn-Sherbok, L. and D. (2001) *Judaism: A Short Reader*. Oxford, OneWorld.

Cole, W.O. and Sambhi, P.S. (1978) *The Sikhs: Their Religious Beliefs and Practices*. London, Routledge and Kegan Paul.

Cragg, K. (1995) *The Event of the Qur'an: Islam in its Scripture*. Oxford, OneWorld.

Dawson, L.L. (2003) *Cults and New Religious Movements: A Reader*. Oxford, Blackwell.

Dumoulin, H. (1994) *Zen Buddhism: A History – India and China*. New York, Macmillan.

Dundas, P. (1992) *The Jains*. London, Routledge.

Eliade, M. (1979) *Patterns in Comparative Religion*. London, Sheed and Ward.

Gibb, H.A.R. (1975) *Islam: A Historical Survey*. London, Oxford University Press.

Hooker, M. (2003) *Paul: A Short Introduction*. Oxford, OneWorld.

Jackson, R. and Nesbitt, E. (1993) *Hindu Children in Britain*. Stoke on Trent, Trentham.

Keown, D. (1992) *The Nature of Buddhist Ethics*. London, Macmillan.

Kirkland, R. (2004) *Taoism: The Enduring Tradition*. London, Routledge.

Ling, T. (1968) *A History of Religion East and West*. London, Macmillan.

Martin, R.C. (2001) *Approaches to Islam in Religious Studies*. Oxford, OneWorld.

Martin, R.C. (1982) *Islam: A Cultural Perspective*. Englewood Cliffs, Prentice-Hall.

Masunaga, R. (1972) *A Primer of Soto Zen*. London, Routledge and Kegan Paul.

McLeod, W.H. (1989) *The Sikhs: History, Religion and Society*. New York, Columbia University Press.

Mittal, S. and Thursby, G. eds. (2004) *The Hindu World*. London, Routledge.

Moore, P. (1982) *Christianity*. London, Ward Lock.

O'Flaherty, W. (1975) *Hindu Myths*. Harmondsworth, Penguin.

O'Flaherty, W.D. (1981) *The Rig Veda*. Harmondsworth, Penguin.

Parrinder, E.G. (1971) *A Dictionary of Non-Christian Religions*. Amersham, Hulton.

Pye, E.M. ed. (1993) *Macmillan Dictionary of Religions*. London, Macmillan.

Rippin, A. (2005) *Muslims: Their Religious Beliefs and Practices*. Third edn. London, Routledge.

Ruthven, M. (1984) *Islam and the World*. London, Penguin.

Saddhatissa, H. (1971) *The Buddha's Way*. London, Allen and Unwin.

Shackle, C. and Mandair, A.S. eds. (2005) *Sikh Scriptures: Selected Readings*. London, Routledge.

Shaw, A. (1988) *A Pakistani Community in Britain*. Oxford, Blackwell.

Sutherland, S. and Clarke, P. eds. (1991) *The Study of Religion: Traditional and New Religions*. London, Routledge.

Suzuki, D.T. (1969) *An Introduction to Zen Buddhism*. London, Rider.

Unterman, A. (1981) *Jews: Their Religious Beliefs and Practices*. London, Routledge.

Walshe, M. (1987) *Thus Have I Heard: The Long Discourses of the Buddha*. London, Wisdom.

Watt, W.M. (1994) *Companion to the Qur'an*. Oxford, OneWorld.

Williams, R.B. (1984) *A New Face of Hinduism*. Cambridge, Cambridge University Press.

Woodhead, L. ed. (2001) *Religions in the Modern World: Traditions and Transformations*. London, Routledge.

Xing, G. (2004) *The Concept of the Buddha*. London, RoutledgeCurzon.

Yandell, K.E. (1999) *Philosophy of Religion*. London, Routledge.

Zablocki, B. and Robbins, T. eds. (2001) *Misunderstanding Cults: Searching for Objectivity in a Controversial Field*. Toronto, University of Toronto Press.

Website addresses

The following sites have been selected because they provide access to a broad range of information on a variety of world faiths.

BBC Religions

http://www.bbc.co.uk/religion/religions

Culham Institute, RE online project

http://www.reonline.org.uk

Intute consortium, Humanities, Religion and theology

http://www.intute.ac.uk/religion

University of Birmingham, Biblical Resources Search

http://www.markgoodacre.org/multibib

University of Birmingham, British Muslims Monthly Survey

http://artsweb.bham.ac.uk/bmms/

University of Cambridge, Centre of South Asian Studies

http://www.s-asian.cam.ac.uk

University of Cumbria, Division of Religion and philosophy

http://philtar.ucsm.ac.uk/

University of Derby, Mult-Faith Centre

http://www.multifaithcentre.org

University of Manchester, British Association for Jewish Studies Bulletin

http://www.bajsbulletin.org

University of Strathclyde, Religious and Moral Education

http://www.strath.ac.uk/Departments/SocialStudies/RE/Database/index.html

Index

Credits